Ò   ML   128   .S6   M8   1973

Muller, Joseph

The Star Spangled Banner.

The Star-Spangled banner.

O say! can you see by the dawn's early light
What so proudly we hail'd at the twilight's last gleaming,
Whose broad stripes and bright stars, through the clouds of the fight,
O'er the ramparts we watch'd were so gallantly streaming?
And the rocket's red glare - the bomb bursting in air
Gave proof through the night that our flag was still there?
O say, does that star-spangled banner yet wave
O'er the land of the free & the home of the brave? —

On that shore, dimly seen through the mists of the deep,
Where the foe's haughty host in dread silence reposes,
What is that, which the breeze, o'er the towering steep
As it fitfully blows, half conceals, half discloses?
Now it catches the gleam — of the morning's first beam,
In full glory reflected, now shines in the stream,
'Tis the Star-spangled banner — O long may it wave
O'er the land of the free & the home of the brave!

And where are the foes that so vauntingly swore
That the havoc of war & the battle's confusion
A home and a Country should leave us no more?
Their blood has wash'd out their foul footstep's pollution.
No refuge could save — the hireling & Slave
From the terror of flight, or the gloom of the grave,
And the Star-spangled banner in triumph doth wave
O'er the land of the free & the home of the brave.

O thus be it ever! when freemen shall stand
Between their lov'd homes & the war's desolation.
Blest with vict'ry & peace, may the heav'n-rescued land
Praise the power that hath made and preserved us a nation.
Then conquer we must — when our cause it is just,
And this be our motto — in God is our trust —
And the Star-spangled banner in triumph shall wave
O'er the land of the free & the home of the brave.

F S Key

Da Capo Press Music Reprint Series
GENERAL EDITOR
FREDERICK FREEDMAN
VASSAR COLLEGE

THE STAR SPANGLED BANNER

FRANCIS SCOTT KEY

(See Note Page 46)

𝔗𝔥𝔢 𝔖𝔱𝔞𝔯 𝔖𝔭𝔞𝔫𝔤𝔩𝔢𝔡 𝔅𝔞𝔫𝔫𝔢𝔯

Words and Music

ISSUED BETWEEN 1814-1864

*An Annotated Bibliographical List
With Notices of the Different Versions, Texts,
Variants, Musical Arrangements, and Notes
on Music Publishers in the United States.*

Illustrated With 108 Portraits, Facsimiles, etc.

Compiled by

JOSEPH MULLER

Supplement by
Lester S. Levy and James J. Fuld

DA CAPO PRESS • NEW YORK • 1973

Library of Congress Cataloging in Publication Data

Muller, Joseph, d. 1939.
    The Star Spangled Banner.

    (Da Capo Press music reprint series)
    1. Star-Spangled Banner—Bibliography.
ML128.S6M8   1973   016.7847'19'73   79-169653
ISBN 0-306-70263-0

This Da Capo Press edition of
The Star Spangled Banner is an
unabridged republication of the 1935 edition
published by G. A. Baker & Co., Inc., New York,
in a printing limited to 500 copies.

The Supplement appeared originally in *Notes* 26/2 (December, 1970) 245—251.
It is reprinted by permission of the authors and of the Music Library Association, Inc.
The final entry of the supplement, No. 69, has been altered by the
authors for this edition.

Published by Da Capo Press, Inc.
A Subsidiary of Plenum Publishing Corporation
227 West 17th Street, New York, New York 10011

TO
TOMMY,
Our Young American

ACKNOWLEDGMENTS

I wish to acknowledge the invaluable services rendered me by Mr. W. Oliver Strunk, now chief of the music division of the Library of Congress; Mr. Louis H. Dielman, librarian of the Peabody Institute and the Maryland Historical Society of Baltimore; Mrs. Margaret M. Mott of the Grosvenor Library at Buffalo and numerous custodians of libraries and institutions, most of whom are mentioned in the "Key" on page 217. The small libraries and institutions as well as the larger ones have generously aided me in assembling the material for this bibliography.

Mr. Malone Bunting Knowles of Yardley, Pa., a direct descendant of Thomas Carr, the original arranger of "The Star Spangled Banner" in music form, has made available particularly valuable first-hand information. Mr. Knowles and his charming wife have thrown open to me their family treasures, supplied transcripts of family documents relating to the original publication of the national anthem and permitted the use of hitherto unpublished portraits of the Carr family.

I am signally grateful to Josiah K. Lilly of Indianapolis, the High Priest of "Foster Hall." Mr. Lilly's encouragement has been most heartening, and he came to my rescue with badly needed imprints which I had despaired of finding.

I wish also to mention especially my good friend Harry McNeill Bland who first started me on collecting American music. His comments and valuable information on the subject have been very helpful.

I am greatly obliged to Mr. Charles J. Nagy of Philadelphia, collector and student of and dealer in rare American music, for helping me gather the material for this work.

My correspondence with Mr. William Arms Fisher of Boston and the use of his *One Hundred and Fifty Years of Music Publishing in the United States,* Boston, 1933, have been of inestimable assistance to me in collecting data on publishers.

Private collectors whom it is my privilege to thank for giving me access to their treasures are: Mr. J. Francis Driscoll of Brookline, Mass., Mr. Arthur Billings Hunt of Brooklyn, N. Y. and Mr. Elliott Shapiro of New York City.

I wish to acknowledge my debt to Dr. Carleton Sprague Smith, chief of the music division of the New York Public Library, for his suggestions and criticism.

I am grateful to Miss Eugenia C. Willig of Baltimore, for allowing me to have a photograph made of the splendid painting of her grandfather, George Willig, Jr., to Miss Helen M. Simonton of Baltimore, for the excellent daguerreotype of her illustrious ancestor, John Cole, and to Mrs. Elizabeth W. Jaquith of East Orange, N. J. for photographs of John Geib Senior and John Geib Junior, her ancestors.

Closter, New Jersey,
December 30, 1934.

J. M.

FOREWORD

Those of us, and there are many, who have profited by Joseph Muller's generous contributions to our books will welcome the publication of a volume of his own. Never has the spirit of the collector and his eagerness to share his discoveries with others been so apparent as it has been with the sage of Closter, New Jersey. Starting as an amateur (in the truest sense of that abused term) Mr. Muller has devoted years of travel and search to assembling one of the outstanding collections of early prints and manuscripts, as well as holograph letters and portraits of musicians. And all the time he has spent hours in his attic retreat at Closter cataloguing and studying his treasures until he has become one of the leading authorities on old music, particularly on that division of old music closest to his affections—"Americana."

It is fortunate that Mr. Muller's first book to be published should be devoted to a highly specialized subject, for he has brought concentrated study to a most important topic—the history of our national anthem in its printed form. This in itself is a significant contribution to American history, for it starts where Oscar G. Sonneck left off in his examination of the origin of the tune and words. Yet there is a broader accomplishment in Mr. Muller's volume than is apparent from its title and its avowed purpose. In his introduction he reviews the field of early music publishing, first in the colonies, and later in the United States; he traces the history of such pioneer figures as the Carrs and other immigrants; and he puts forever at rest some false traditions about our national anthem.

All of this is accomplished with painstaking thoroughness and a remarkable scholarliness, yet withal there is apparent on every page the intense love the author has for his subject, an affection which renders the work human and readable. I for one cannot conceive of Joseph Muller becoming dry, even when he compiles a scholarly bibliography.

It is therefore a privilege to be allowed a small part in launching such an excellent book written by a friend who has contributed so much to the books on American music. I sincerely hope that every library in the nation, and every private collector of old music, will find a place for it, where it will be available to all who seek information about the "Star Spangled Banner."

JOHN TASKER HOWARD

CONTENTS

		Page
Acknowledgments		3
Foreword		5
List of Illustrations		9
Introduction		11
The Carrs		39
Bibliography		47
Key		217
Index		219
Supplement		225

LIST OF ILLUSTRATIONS

FRANCIS SCOTT KEY   *Frontispiece*

ADAMS AND LIBERTY. Published by G. Gilfert, New York, (1798–1801).   16–17

ADAMS AND LIBERTY. From a Ms. Copy in a Bound Book owned by Eleanor Parke
  Custis, 1798.   18–19

WHEN DEATH'S GLOOMY ANGEL WAS BENDING HIS BOW. Anacreontic Adaptation published ca. 1813.   21–22

DEFENCE OF FORT M'HENRY. Early Broadside.   24

THE STAR SPANGLED BANNER. English and German Texts. Ca. 1861.   26

THE STAR SPANGLED BANNER. Parody Published in the *Temperance Annual and
  Cold Water Magazine*. 1843.   30

THE PILLAR OF GLORY. Published in the *Port Folio*, November, 1813.   32–33

FACSIMILE OF ORIGINAL BILL DECLARING "THE STAR SPANGLED BAN-
  NER" THE NATIONAL ANTHEM.   37

TITLE-PAGE OF JOSEPH CARR'S SALE CATALOGUE, London, February 14, 1794.   38

JOSEPH CARR   40

THOMAS CARR   43

EXCERPTS FROM THE CORRESPONDENCE OF MARY JORDAN CARR.   44–45

THE STAR SPANGLED BANNER. Published by Joseph Carr, Baltimore. *First Edition.* 50–51

THE BATTLE OF THE WABASH. Published by G. E. Blake, Philadelphia.   53

THE BATTLE OF THE WABASH. Published by G. E. Blake, Philadelphia. *Amended
  Edition.*   54–55–56

THE STAR SPANGLED BANNER. Published by J. Carr, Baltimore. *Amended Edition.* 59–60

STAR SPANGLED BANNER. Published by A. Bacon & Co., Philadelphia.   62–63

JOHN GEIB, Sr.   65

JOHN GEIB, Jr.   66

STAR SPANGLED BANNER. Published by Thomas Carr, Baltimore.   68–69

STAR SPANGLED BANNER. Published by George Willig, Baltimore.   72

GEORGE WILLIG, Jr.   74

JOHN COLE   76

THE STAR SPANGLED BANNER. Published by John Cole, Baltimore.   77–78

TITLE-PAGE OF "BUY A BROOM." Published by John Cole, Baltimore, ca. 1835.
  Showing John Cole's Music Store.   79

THE STAR SPANGLED BANNER. Published by Firth and Hall, New York.   81–82–83

JOHN FIRTH. THE FIRTH, POND & CO. BUILDING, No. 1, Franklin Square, New
  York.   85

THE STAR SPANGLED BANNER. Published by Atwill, New York.   92–93–94–95

TITLE-PAGE OF "BROADWAY SIGHTS." Published by Atwill, New York, 1835.
  Showing Atwill's Establishment, No. 201 Broadway.   97

FRANCIS H. BROWN. TITLE-PAGE OF I'LL LOVE THEE IN THE SPRING
  TIME." Published by William Hall & Son, New York, 1856.   98

THE STAR SPANGLED BANNER. Published by Oliver Ditson, Boston.   105–106–107

OLIVER DITSON   108

THE STAR SPANGLED BANNER. Published by Jollie, New York.   110

STAR SPANGLED BANNER. Published by Oliver Ditson & Co., Boston. (Reissue from the J. L. Peters & Bro., St. Louis Edition.)   113–114–115–116

THE STAR SPANGLED BANNER. Published by D'Almaine & Co., London.   120

THE STAR SPANGLED BANNER. Published by C. Sheard; The Musical Bouquet Office, London.   121

THE WILLIAM HALL & SON BUILDING, No. 239 Broadway, New York.   125

STAR SPANGLED BANNER. Published by Oliver Ditson, Boston.   127–128

STAR SPANGLED BANNER. Published by William Hall & Son, New York.   130–131–132–133

STAR SPANGLED BANNER. Published by A. C. Peters & Sons, Cincinnati.   135

STAR SPANGLED BANNER. Published by A. C. Peters & Bro., Cincinnati.   137

TITLE–PAGE OF "HIGHLANDERS' MARCH." Published by A. C. & J. L. Peters, Cincinnati, 1860. Showing the A. C. & J. L. Peters Music Store in Cincinnati.   138

STAR SPANGLED BANNER. Published by R. Wittig, Philadelphia.   141–142–143–144

STAR SPANGLED BANNER. Published by Lee & Walker, Philadelphia.   147–148–149–150

STAR SPANGLED BANNER. Published by Lee & Walker, Philadelphia.   152

STAR SPANGLED BANNER. Published by Oliver Ditson & Co., Boston.   156

TITLE–PAGE OF THE "COSTUME POLKA." With view of the Lee & Walker Establishment.   158

STAR SPANGLED BANNER. Published by Blodgett & Bradford, Buffalo.   160

STAR SPANGLED BANNER AND THE AMERICAN FLAG. Published by Blodgett & Bradford, Buffalo.   163

STAR SPANGLED BANNER. Published by John Church, Jr., Cincinnati.   166

STAR SPANGLED BANNER. Published by William Dressler, New York.   169

WILLIAM DRESSLER.   170

TITLE–PAGE OF "THOU HAST LEARNED TO LOVE ANOTHER." Showing view of Oliver Ditson & Co.'s Establishment.   172

STAR SPANGLED BANNER. Published by C. Breusing, New York.   176

STAR SPANGLED BANNER. Published by S. T. Gordon, New York.   178

STEPHEN THAYER GORDON.   179

STAR SPANGLED BANNER. Published by Oliver Ditson & Co., Boston.   188–189–190–191

STAR SPANGLED BANNER. Published by Russell & Tolman, Boston.   194–195–196–197

STAR SPANGLED BANNER. Published by Russell & Tolman, Boston.   200

HENRY TOLMAN.   202

TITLE–PAGE of "EXCELSIOR POLKA." Showing view of Russell & Tolman's Establishment, Boston.   203

STAR SPANGLED BANNER. Published by S. Brainard & Co., Cleveland.   205–206–207–208

STAR SPANGLED BANNER. Published by G. André & Co., Philadelphia.   211–212–213–214

INTRODUCTION

1

The history of the innumerable patriotic songs of the United States is a lively and vivid chronicle of the United States itself. The most important of them, our national anthem, "The Star-Spangled Banner," has had interesting bibliographical adventures. During years of collecting American musical imprints, the writer has come across hundreds of patriotic sheet-music publications, in both vocal and instrumental form, ranging in date of publication from about 1793 to the present day. Among these were original song-sheet issues of "The Star-Spangled Banner" hitherto entirely unknown, and these finds have been supplemented by other discoveries about the song which are well worth setting down.

Apparently no bibliography of the words and music of "The Star-Spangled Banner" has yet been compiled. This first attempt to trace the early editions of the anthem is necessarily subject to future corrections and additions. It is limited to editions published in sheet-music form through the period of fifty years from 1814, when it was written, until 1864, when its popularity was assured. A history of the words and music, a study of the variations in editions and musical arrangements, considerable information about the publishers, descriptions of the pictorial covers and other items of interest have been included. No attempt has been made, however, to cover the innumerable issues of the song in song-books of the period or the various imitations, adaptations and parodies which flooded the country. Even in the field to which the writer has limited himself, the material is so scattered that it is impossible to claim absolute completeness. Many early editions and much valuable material are undoubtedly packed away in old trunks and mouldering in garrets.

In pre-Revolutionary days the amount of secular music written and published in America was negligible and sporadic. Song-hits and popular instrumental pieces from ballad-operas, pantomimes and the like, as well as the classical music performed by itinerant opera troupes and orchestras in the larger cities along the Atlantic seacoast, were largely imported from England and sold in book-shops and general stores.

The first patriotic song, and probably the earliest sheet-music printed in the colonies was issued in broadside form. It was called "A Song for American Freedom," written in 1768 by John Dickinson of Boston to the tune of "Hearts of Oak," and printed and published (with music) by Mein and Fleming in Boston, in September, 1768, as "The Liberty Song." Unfortunately no copy of it seems to be extant. A second text of it was printed in 1768 by Hall and Sellers of Philadelphia as a broadside without music. Mein and Fleming again published it with music in *Bickerstaff's Boston Almanac,* 1769.

The ballad broadsides which were called into service during the Revolution and enjoyed considerable popularity just after the founding of the Republic, developed, in the course of half a century, into the campaign-broadsides which played a prominent part in later presidential elections.

Broadsides began to appear with printed verses commemorative of current historical events marked with the names of the popular airs to which the lines were to be sung or occasionally printed with music. Naturally, little value was attached to these leaflets, which were published for cheap or free distribution, so that few have survived.

The earliest secular music printed in America first appeared in magazines and periodicals, beginning in 1774 and continuing up to about 1791. During the actual period of the Revolution little of this music was published, but an extensive revival of it followed the proclamation of peace. The *American Magazine*, the *Boston Magazine,* the *Columbia Magazine,* the *Massachusetts Magazine,* the *New York Magazine,* the *Pennsylvania Magazine* and several others featured musical compositions in their monthly issues. This material comprised musical dissertations and poems with indications of the tunes to which they were to be sung, and a great number of popular ballads and patriotic songs with words and music. The first piece of music to appear in these magazines was "The Hill Tops; A New Hunting Song," the words and music engraved by Joseph Callender, and published in the April number of the *Royal American Magazine,* Vol. I, Boston, 1774. The first attempt in the patriotic vein was the "Death of General Wolfe," a subject which was repeatedly used in broadsides. The *Pennsylvania Magazine* printed this song with piano accompaniment, engraved by J. Smithers, in its number for March, 1775. The *Massachusetts Magazine,* which published more musical pieces than any of the others, carried several "odes" in honor of General Washington written between 1789 and 1791.

More important in the musical history of the United States than these occasional publications, however, are such men as Alexander Reinagle, George Schetky, Raynor Taylor, Gottlieb Graupner, Robert Shaw, the Carr family, George Willig, and the other musicians and music publishers who emigrated to the new country during the last fifteen years of the eighteenth century to settle here and pursue their chosen professions. Although music publishing was already established as a separate business, a number of these newcomers conducted their own music-shops, writing and publishing their works themselves. Their publications, like all the printed music of the period, were, both typographically and in general appearance, in the English style of music-printing. Many of these were reprints from the ballad-operas of Arne, Dibdin, Shield, Hook, Storace and other British composers, and others were instrumental pieces and patriotic songs.

An invaluable bibliographical resumé of the secular music published in the eighteenth century, compiled by O. G. T. Sonneck under the title: "Early Secular American Music," [1] has become a text-book for collectors and scholars. The only available records of musical publications after 1800, however, are those housed in the Library of Congress and in certain libraries and historical institutions scattered throughout the country. Recent widespread interest and research in this field fortunately has brought to light much valuable information.

A difficult and delicate piece of detective work, which every collector thoroughly enjoys, is necessary to determine the exact date on which each of these old pieces

---

[1] Sonneck, O. G.; *Early Secular American Music* 1905.

of music appeared in print. In many cases it is an impossible task. Until the 1830's it was not customary to date musical publications and, although the original copyright act: "An act for the encouragement of learning by securing the copies of maps, charts, and books to the authors and proprietors of such copies during the times therein mentioned," was passed by Congress as early as 1790, very few writers and composers took advantage of the protection. Raynor Taylor's "The Kentucky Volunteer," deposited January 6, 1794, is said to be the earliest deposit in the Library of Congress, but the practice of copyrighting did not really come into popular use until the 'thirties and was not universally adopted before the middle of the century.

One of the oldest and most reliable methods for discovering the date of an uncopyrighted publication is the careful scanning of old newspapers for advertisements announcing the publications of various publishers. The advertisements, of course, give the street address of the publisher, and this information, added to the date of issue of the newspaper, establishes the location of the publisher at a specific period. Comparison of publishers' addresses found in old city directories with the firm name and address in the publishers' imprint line on the publication often furnishes the date of a music sheet within a period of a few years. Some publishers numbered their imprints with consecutive plate numbers which usually can be compared with copyrighted editions to fix the date of appearance. Occasionally the engraver's name gives the clue. In many cases there are still other ways of solving the problem and the collector's ingenuity is constantly taxed, to his everlasting delight.

2

The air to which "The Star-Spangled Banner" is sung had its origin in England. Some time in the second half of the eighteenth century a convivial club, known as the Anacreontic Society, was formed in London. Meetings were held regularly at the Crown and Anchor Tavern in the Strand, and musical entertainment, in which professionals were invited to participate, was a part of the program. Supper was served after the concert and then all the members joined in choral singing. The singing was always opened with the club's constitutional song, "To Anacreon in Heaven," written some time between 1771 and 1776 by its president Ralph Tomlinson. The earliest appearance of the text in printed form is in Number IV of *The Vocal Magazine, or British Songster's Miscellany* . . . London, Printed by J. Harrison for J. Bew, 1778, as follows:

ANACREONTIC SOCIETY

Written by Ralph Tomlinson, Esq.

To Anacreon in Heav'n, where he sat in full glee,
    A few sons of harmony sent a petition,
That he their inspirer and patron would be;
    When this answer arriv'd from the jolly old Grecian—

[13]

Voice, fiddle, and flute,
No longer be mute;
I'll lend ye my name, and inspire ye to boot:
And besides, I'll instruct ye, like me, to intwine
The myrtle of Venus with Bacchus's vine.

The news through Olympus immediately flew;
When old Thunder pretended to give himself airs—
If these mortals are suffer'd their scheme to pursue,
The devil a goddess will stay above stairs.
Hark! already they cry,
In transports of joy,
A fig for Parnassus! to Rowley's we'll fly;
And there my good fellows, we'll learn to intwine
The myrtle of Venus with Bacchus's vine.

The yellow-hair'd god, and his nine fusty maids,
To the hill of old Lud will incontinent flee,
Idalia will boast but of tenantless shàdes,
And the biforked hill a mere desert will be.
My thunder, no fear on't,
Will soon do its errand,
And dam'me! I'll swinge the ringleaders, I warrant.
I'll trim the young dogs, for thus daring to twine
The myrtle of Venus with Bacchus's vine.

Apollo rose up; and said, Pr'ythee ne'er quarrel,
Good King of the gods, with my vot'ries below!
Your thunder is useless—then, shewing his laurel,
Cry'd, Sic evitabile fulmen, you know!
Then over each head
My laurels I'll spread;
So my sons from your crackers no mischief shall dread,
Whilst snug in their club-room, they jovially twine
The myrtle of Venus with Bacchus's vine.

Next Momus got up, with his risable phiz,
And swore with Apollo he'd chearfully join—
The full tide of harmony still shall be his,
But the song and the catch, and the laugh shall be mine:
Then, Jove, be not jealous
Of these honest fellows.
Cry'd Jove, We relent, since the truth you now tell us;
And swear by Old Styx, that they long shall intwine
The myrtle of Venus with Bacchus's vine.

[14]

Ye sons of Anacreon, then, join hand in hand;
   Preserve unanimity, friendship, and love.
'Tis your's to support what's so happily plan'd;
   You've the sanction of gods, and the fiat of Jove.
               While thus we agree,
               Our toast let it be.
   May our club flourish happy, united, and free!
   And long may the sons of Anacreon intwine
   The myrtle of Venus with Bacchus's vine.

Sonneck furnishes what is apparently conclusive [2] proof that another member of the society, one John Stafford Smith, originally composed the music now thoroughly familiar to us as the air of our national anthem. Smith, according to Grove's *Dictionary of Music and Musicians,* was an "able organist, an efficient tenor singer, an excellent composer and an accomplished antiquary." The peculiar melodic structure of the piece is due partly to the irregular form of the poem and partly, perhaps, to demands from the society's more ambitious members for a tune which would exploit their vocal range. Despite these handicaps, the public seems to have taken immediately to the tune and it appeared in the song-books of the day. "To Anacreon in Heaven," generally known as "The Anacreontic Song," as actually sung by the society, probably originated about the year 1775, according to Sonneck, and was first published in sheet-music form by Longman and Broderip, London music publishers, sometime between 1780 and 1783.[3]

The popularity of "To Anacreon in Heaven" in England, where it appeared in many editions, was soon transferred to America. "Anacreontic" societies were founded in imitation of the London original, and immigrant singers performed the music until it became one of the most familiar airs of the day. Native poetasters were continually fitting new words to the tune, usually in celebration of some patriotic theme. The earliest of these adaptations extant is in the *Columbian Songster,* New York, 1797 (p. 136). "Song: For the glorious Fourteenth of July" ("The Genius of France from his star begem'd throne . . ."). Literally dozens of patriotic poems, written to the tune of this "jolly song" appear in early song-books between 1797 and the time when Francis Scott Key wrote his immortal lines (1814). Sonneck, in his *Report* on the

_____

[2] Sonneck, O. G. T.; *The Star Spangled Banner (Revised and enlarged from the "Report" on above and other airs, issued in 1909).*   1914

This erudite and definite work, compiled while the author was chief of the music division at the Library of Congress, is indispensable to the student of the history of the national anthem. The writer of this article is greatly indebted to it for information on the subject.

[3] Sonneck, O. G. T.; *The Star Spangled Banner,* 1914. Here, on pages 42–44, the date of publication of this issue is critically and thoroughly examined, and the Longman and Broderip imprints of "The Anacreontic Song" are reproduced. (See: plates VIII and IX.)

The date, however, may safely be narrowed down to 1779–1780 by examination and careful checking of a catalogue of "Longman and Broderip ,Music-sellers to the Royal Family, at the King's Arms and Apollo, No. 26, Cheapside, London", a copy of which was recently acquired by the writer and is now owned by the Library of Congress. On page 13 of this undated, 16 page, octavo size pamphlet appears (for the first time, probably,) "The Anacreontic Song" listed among "Vocal Music. English Songs, &c."

[15]

ADAMS AND LIBERTY
Published by G. Gilfert, New York. (1798–1801)

(2)

In a clime whose Vales feed the marts of the world,
Whose Shores are Unshaken by Europes Commotion,
The Trident of Commerce should never be hurl'd,
To Incence the Legitimate Powers of the Ocean.
But should Pirates invade,
Though in Thunder array'd,
Let your Cannon declare the free charter of Trade.
For Ne'er &c.

(3)

The fame of our arms, of our Laws the mild sway,
Had Justly Ennobled our Nation in story,
Till the dark clouds of Faction obscur'd our young day
And Envelop'd the sun of American Glory.
But let Traitors be told,
Who their Country have sold,
And Barter'd their God, for his Image in Gold.
That Ne'er &c.

(4)

While France her huge limbs bathes recumbent in blood,
And Society's Base threats with wide Dissolution,
May peace, like the dove, who Return'd from the flood,
Find an Ark of abode in our mild Constitution.
But peace in our aim,
Yet the boon we disclaim,
IF Bought by our Sov'reignty, justice, and Fame.
For Ne'er &c.

(5)

Tis the Fire of the Flint each American warms,
Let Rome's haughty Victors, beware of Collision,
Let them bring all the Vassals of Europe in Arms,
We're a World by Ourselves and disdain a Division
While with Patriots pride,
To our Laws were allied,
No Foe can subdue us, no Faction Divide.
For Ne'er &c.

(6)

Our Mountains are Crown'd with Imperial Oak,
Whose roots, like our Liberties, Ages have Nourish'd,
But long ere our Nation submits to the Yoke,
Not a tree shall be left on the Field where it Flourish'd.
Should Invasion Impenl,
Ev'ry grove would Descend,
From the hill tops they shaded our Shores to Defend
For Ne'er &c.

(7)

Let our Patriots destroy Anarch's Pestilents worm,
Lest our Liberty's growth should be Check'd by Corrosion,
Then Let Clouds thicken round we heed not the storm,
Our realm fears no Shock, but the Earth's own Explosion
Toes Assail us in vain,
Though their fleets bridge the main,
For our Altars and Laws with our lives weel maintain
And Ne'er &c.

(8)

Should the tempest of war over shadow our land,
Its bolt could ne'er rend Freedoms Temple Asunder,
For unmov'd as its Portal, would WASHINGTON stand,
And Repulse, with his breast the Assaults of the thunder
For his Sword from the sleep
Of its scabbard would leap
And Conduct with its point every flash to the deep
For Ne'er &c.

(9)

Let Fame to the world sound America's Voice,
No Intrigue can her Sons from their Goverment sever,
Her pride is her ADAMS, his Laws are her Choice,
And Shall flourish till Liberty Slumbers for ever,
Then Unite heart and hand,
Like Leonidas' band,
And Swear to the God of the Ocean and Land.
That Ne'er &c.

ADAMS AND LIBERTY
Published by G. Gilfert, New York. (1798–1801)

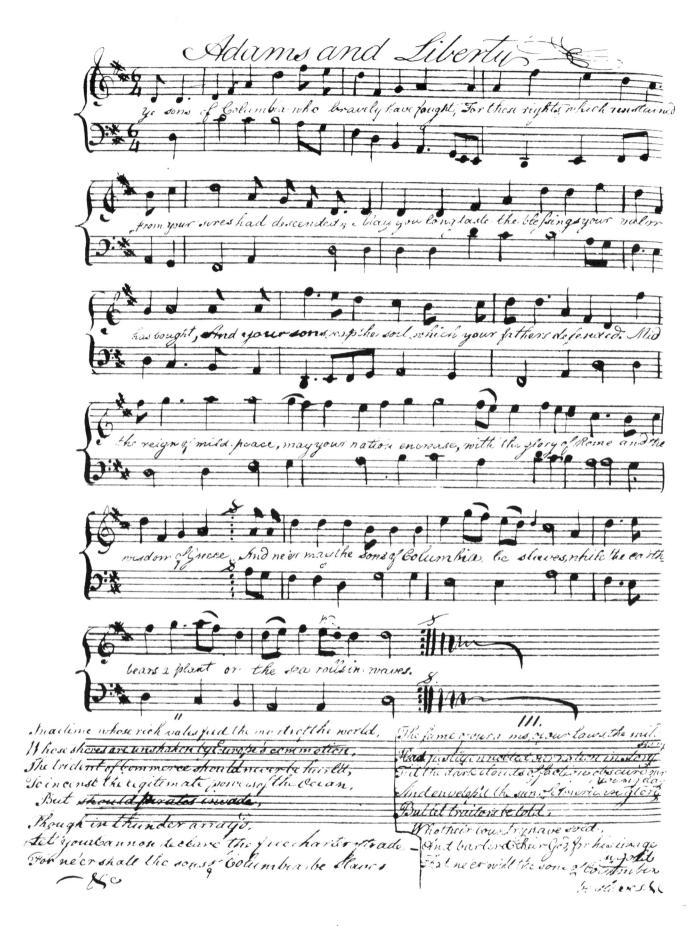

ADAMS AND LIBERTY
From a Manuscript Copy in a Bound Book of Music owned by Eleanor Parke Custis, 1798.

IV.

When France her huge limbs bathes recumbent in blood,
And society's base threats with wide dissolution,
May peace, like the dove, who return'd from the flood,
Find an Ark of abode in our mild constitution
But though peace is our aim,
yet the boon we disclaim,
If bought by our sovereignty, justice or fame: For ne'er shall the sons of Columbia

V.

In the fire of the flint each American warms;
Let Rome's... vainly beware of the collision,
Let them bring all the vassals of Europe in arms,
We're a world by ourselves— and disdain a division!
While with patriot pride,
To our laws we're allied
No foe can subdue us, no faction divide,   For ne'er &c &c &c

VI.

Our mountains are crown'd with Imperial oak,
Whose roots, like our liberties, ages have nourish'd;
But e'er our nation submits to the yoke,
Not a tree shall be left on the field where it flourish'd.
Should invasion impend, ev'ry grove would descend,
From the hilltops they shaded our shores to defend.   For ne'er shall the sons of Columbia &c &c

VII.

Let our Patriots destroy Anarch's pestilent worm,
Lest our Liberty's growth should be check'd by corrosion;
Then let clouds thicken round us, we heed not the storm,
Our realms feel no shock, but the earth's own explosion.
Foes assail'd us in vain, Though their fleets bridge the main,
For our Altars and laws with our lives we'll maintain.   Then ne'er shall the sons of Columbia &c &c

VIII

Should the tempest of war overshadow our land,
Its bolts could ne'er rend freedom's temple asunder,
For unmov'd at its portal would Washington stand,
And repulse, with his breast, the assaults of the thunder!
His sword from the sleep, of its scabbard would leap,
And conduct with its point ev'ry flash to the deep.   For ne'er shall the sons of Columbia &c &c

IX.

Let Fame to the world sound America's voice;
No intrigue can her sons from their government sever,
Her pride is her Adams— his laws are her choice,
And shall flourish— till Liberty slumber forever
Then unite heart and hand, like Leonidas' band
And swear to the God of the Ocean and Land,
That ne'er shall the sons of Columbia be slaves,
While the Earth bears a plant, or the Sea rolls in waves.

ADAMS AND LIBERTY
From a Manuscript Copy in a Bound Book of Music owned by Eleanor Parke Custis, 1798.

origin of our national airs,[4] lists over twenty, many of which the writer has seen, and this list is by no means complete.

Robert Treat Paine, the son of one of the signers of the Declaration of Independence, made the most famous early adaptation of the tune. His poem, "Adams and Liberty" ("Ye sons of Columbia who bravely have fought . ."), written for an anniversary of the Massachusetts Charitable Fire Society of Boston, was known as "The Boston Patriotic Song" and was first sung in Boston on June 1, 1798. It had an instantaneous success and on the day following its debut was printed from the press of Thomas & Andrews of Boston.[5]

Another scarce and interesting Anacreontic offshoot is a song, "When Death's gloomy Angel was bending his bow," written in 1813 in commemoration of Washington's death for the first anniversary of the Washington Benevolent Society of Pennsylvania. The music was arranged by Raynor Taylor and published by George Willig of Philadelphia. (See plates 3 and 3a.)

---

[4] Sonneck, O. G. T.; Report on *The Star-Spangled Banner, Hail Columbia, America, Yankee Doodle*. 1909

[5] Thomas & Andrews, the Boston printers, who are credited with having been one of the earliest firms to import music type to America, were first to print and issue the song according to an advertisement in the *Columbian Sentinel*, May 30, 1798, quoted in L. C. Elson's *History of American Music*, 1904, page 151. The copy of "Adams and Liberty. | The Boston Patriotic Song. | Written by Thomas Paine, A. M." in the *American Antiquarian Society* at Worcester is unquestionably one of these issues. It is printed on two inside pages on laid paper, watermarked with heraldic figure, the word "Badgen" and the date of "1797". Beneath the title is written in ink in the handwriting of Thomas the memorandum: "Boston. Printed by Thomas & Andrews." Copies of this scarce sheet-song, but without the writing, are in the Boston Public Library and in the New York Public Library.

"Adams and Liberty" appeared in New York in August 1798 with the notation: "Printed & Sold by W. Howe Organ Builder & Importer of all kinds of Musical Instruments, No. 320 Pearl Street" and was advertised as "just published." James Hewitt of 131 William Street, New York, also issued an edition in 1798. A "second edition-corrected" was brought out by Linley & Moore of Boston, and between May 1799 and November, 1800, P. A. von Hagen & Co., Boston, printed a "third edition corrected."

Another edition in the writer's collection was published in New York between 1798 and 1801 by "G. Gilfert at his Musical Magazine No. 177 Broadway." It is embellished with a bust portrait of President John Adams finely engraved on the plate with the music and printed with it. (In those days portraits on music sheets usually were pasted down and mounted in their respective places.) (See: plate 1.)

The song was a familiar one at Mount Vernon before the end of 1798 judging by a volume of music which lately passed through the writer's hands and is now in the Library of Congress. The book, formerly owned by Eleanor Parke Custis, the adopted grand-daughter of George Washington, bears her autograph in several places on the flyleaf, and the date "1798." Among its contents are instrumental numbers, early Philadelphia imprints and handwritten copies of favorite pieces of the period. One of these copies is "Adams and Liberty," evidently made by an amateur, possibly Nelly Custis herself.

Curiously enough, this holograph is not copied from the current version of "Adams and Liberty," but from an issue of "To Anacreon in Heaven." While the American version of the old English tune is written in the key of C major in 3/4 time and differs somewhat from the latter in its musical treatment, the Custis manuscript is in D major, in 6/4 time and of the standard musical form employed in "To Anacreon in Heaven."

Examination of English editions shows the transcript to have been made from either "The Anacreontic Song" published by Anne Lee, Dublin, ca. 1788, or "The Anacreontic Song" printed in *Exshaw's London Magazine*, Dublin, 1791. (See: plates 2 and 2a.) (See: Sonneck; plates III and VII.)

[20]

"WHEN DEATH'S GLOOMY ANGEL WAS BENDING HIS BOW"
Anacreontic Adaptation published ca. 1813.

_ istence u _ _ _ ni _ ted with mine.

2.

With a smile he replied   What shall Washington claim
Exemption from fate, now denied to creation.
Shall his life be immortal and stand like his fame.
The world is unworthy so proud a donation.
    Earth cannot requite,
    A glory so bright:
He seeks from his nature the mansions of light.
Then cease, lovely mourner, to grieve that he flies
A worth so transcendent belongs to the skies.

3.

Then swift flew the shaft and the patriot fell;
    The genius astonished beheld the translation,
For full on her eyes, O how wondrous to tell.
    Burst forth in a moment a bright constellation.
    In the midst, how serene.
    An Angel was seen,
    She gazed, and recognised her Washington's mien
His eye the mild beams of compassion expressed.
While thus the fair mourner the Hero addressed _

4.

Lament not for me _ dry the tears from thy cheek
    For I had with years and with honour grown hoary,
Be silent and treasure the words which I speak
    Before I ascend to the mansions of glory.
    When Faction's rude hand,
    Shall rule o'er thy land,
    A guardian Angel, shall Washington stand;
His eye shall watch o'er thee when dangers impend,
His councils shall guide thee _ his buckler defend.

5.

Should Albion molest in the pride of her sway,
    And once more forsake law and justice for plunder
My spirit shall light on thy Heroes that day,
    Whose hands shall triumphantly brandish thy thunder
    Henceforth on the Sea,
    Thy fates shall decree,
    Hail, Jones, and Decatur shall represent me
On them in full lustre my glory shall shine
And Bainbridge shall mingle his triumphs with mine.

6.

Be undaunted and firm, and confide in my arm,
    Revere thine own self and all nations shall fear thee
And should tyrants abroad, or domestick alarm,
    Then trust that your Guardian Angel is near thee
    Now to regions of light
    I hasten my flight,
    My lasts word are Liberty, Justice, and Right _
He said, and while speaking, from earth he withdrew,
And hid in his cloudy pavilion from view.

"WHEN DEATH'S GLOOMY ANGEL WAS BENDING HIS BOW"
Anacreontic Adaptation published ca. 1813.

With all this evidence one may assume that the air of the well-known drinking song was thoroughly associated in Key's mind with patriotic inspiration. On this point Sonneck says: "Key, when his imagination took fire from the bombardment of Fort McHenry, had either the meter and form of the words and air of "To Anacreon in Heaven" or one of its American offshoots in mind as a scaffold."

3

Francis Scott Key was born on August 9, 1780, at Pipe's Creek, in Frederick County, Maryland, the son of Lieutenant John Ross Key, late of the First Maryland Revolutionary Artillery. About 1801, young Key began the practice of law in Frederick, Maryland, and in the following year married Mary Taloe Lloyd. Eight years later he went to live in Georgetown, D. C., where under the patronage of an uncle, Philip Barton Key, he became District Attorney for the District of Columbia, an office which he held until 1817. During his residence in Georgetown, Key lived at what is now No. 3153 Bridge (or "M") Street. This house is now being converted into the Francis Scott Key Memorial Home.

Key was a devout christian and a prominent member of his church. He was noted at the time for his hymns, many of which show considerable literary merit. "Before The Lord We Bow," and "Lord, With Glowing Heart I Praise Thee" are two of the foremost. Some of his hymns appeared in sheet-music form in a collection entitled: *Lyra Sacra,* published by Miller and Osbourn, Philadelphia, 1832. "The Home of the Soul," written and adapted to the air "Home, Sweet Home," is one of his most interesting contributions to this collection.

Key died in Baltimore on January 11, 1843, and was buried in Mount Olivet Cemetery, Frederick, Maryland. On Flag Day, 1898, a beautiful monument was erected over his remains.

The first and apparently the only authentic story of the origin of "The Star-Spangled Banner" has been handed down to us in Key's own narrative, related shortly after the unsuccessful bombardment of Fort McHenry, to his brother-in-law R. B. Taney, subsequently Chief Justice of the Supreme Court.[6]

On the way to its base after the battle of Bladensburg, the British army passed through the town of Upper Marlborough. A number of stragglers dropped out of the enemy ranks and stayed behind in the town, where their marauding seriously disturbed the populace. Dr. William Beanes, the town physician, and a friend of Key's, organized a small group of citizens to pursue the offenders and take them prisoner. When the British heard of the doctor's activities they promptly seized him and held him a prisoner of war on board their fleet. Key, apprised of his friend's misfortune, hastened to get permission to board the English flag ship and intercede for Beanes' release. He set out from Baltimore in company with John S. Skinner, the commissioner of exchange of prisoners, on the cartel ship "Minden," flying a flag of truce. Admiral Cochrane received the men cordially, and Key, citing Dr. Beanes' former

---

[6] Sonneck; *The Star Spangled Banner* pp. 66–72. This account is here carefully examined and reprinted in part.

DEFENCE OF FORT M'HENRY.

☞ [The annexed song was composed under the following circumstances—A gentleman (*Francis S. Key, Esq. of Georgetown, District of Columbia.*) had left Baltimore, in a flag of truce for the purpose of getting released from the British fleet, a friend of his who had been captured at Marlborough.—He went as far as the mouth of the Patuxent and was not permitted to return lest the intended attack on Baltimore should be disclosed. He was therefore brought up the Bay to the mouth of the Patapsco, where the flag vessel was kept under the guns of a frigate, and he was compelled to witness the bombardment of Fort M'Henry, which the Admiral had boasted that he would carry in a few hours, and that the city must fall. He watched the flag at the Fort through the whole day with an anxiety that can be better felt than described, until the night prevented him from seeing it. In the night he watched the bomb shells, and at early dawn his eye was again greeted by the proudly waving flag of his country.]

Tune—ANACREON IN HEAVEN.

O! SAY can you see by the dawn's early light,   [ing,
  What so proudly we hailed at the twilight's last gleam-
Whose broad stripes and bright stars through the peri-
          lous fight,   [ing ?
  O'er the ramparts we watch'd were so gallantly stream-
And the rockets' red glare, the bombs bursting in air,
Gave proof through the night that our flag was still there;
    O! say does that star-spangled banner yet wave,
      O'er the land of the free, and the home of the brave?

On the shore dimly seen through the mists of the deep,
  Where the foe's haughty host in dread silence reposes,
What is that which the breeze, o'er the towering steep,
  As it fitfully blows, half conceals, half discloses?
Now it catches the gleam of the morning's first beam,
In full glory reflected now shines in the stream.
    'Tis the star-spangled banner, O! long may it wave
      O'er the land of the free, and the home of the brave.

And where is that band who so vauntingly swore
  That the havoc of war and the battle's confusion,
A home and a country, shall leave us no more?
  Their blood has wash'd out their foul footsteps pollution;
No refuge could save the hireling and slave,
From the terror of flight, or the gloom of the grave;
    And the star-spangled banner in triumph doth wave,
      O'er the land of the free, and the home of the brave.

O! thus be it ever when freemen shall stand,
  Between their lov'd home, and the war's desolation,
Blest with vict'ry and peace, may the Heav'n rescued
          land,   [nation !
  Praise the Power that hath made and preserved us a
Then conquer we must, when our cause it is just,
And this be our motto---"*In God is our Trust;*"
    And the star-spangled banner in triumph shall wave,
      O'er the land of the free and the home of the brave.

DEFENCE OF FORT M'HENRY. EARLY BROADSIDE
(Courtesy of Mr. F. G. Sweet, New York City).

generous care of wounded British officers, was able to secure his friend's release. Meanwhile the British had sailed up the Patapsco and had anchored off Fort McHenry in preparation for an attack on Baltimore. Because of this scheme all three Americans were held prisoners lest they give information that would spoil the plan. On the morning of September 13th, while the enemy prepared for the attack, the three men were transferred to their own vessel the "Minden," and held there under guard throughout the bombardment of Fort McHenry which lasted all through the day and the following night. During the night the wildest confusion reigned. Baltimore was shaken to its foundations, the air was heavy with smoke and the river choked with wreckage. Finally, in the early hours of the morning the cannonading suddenly ceased, and at daybreak the three uninvited spectators observed that the British had withdrawn, having failed to carry out their plan, and that the American flag was still flying over the ramparts. It was this scene that inspired the poet then and there to draft his immortal lines.

Key and his friends were soon able to land and to learn the full particulars of the unsuccessful attack. On his way to shore Key finished the poem and on the night he reached Baltimore he wrote it out in its present form. On the next day he showed it to a relative of his, Judge Nicholson, one of the defenders of Fort McHenry, who had a broadside of the poem printed and circulated a few days later. It was headed: "Defence of Fort M'Henry," and "To Anacreon in Heaven" was indicated as the tune to which the words were to be sung.[7] About a week later the handbill was copied

[7] Sonneck; *The Star Spangled Banner*. The broadside and the first completed draft of the poem are here fully described and reproduced (Plates XV and XVI). Both pieces were originally owned by Judge Nicholson and eventually became the property of Mr. Henry Walters of Baltimore. After the latter's death they came under the auctioneer's hammer, but were bought back in the sale at the American Art Association, on January 5, 1934 for the Walters Museum at Baltimore.

An early and hitherto unknown handbill in the possession of Mr. F. G. Sweet of New York, has recently come to the writer's attention. At first glance it looks exactly like the Nicholson-Walters copy, but closer examination brings to light certain small differences. Mr. Sweet's copy is about two inches longer than the other and is set within an ornamental border while the other is plain. The text is the same except that a number of letters set in capitals in the Nicholson-Walters copy have been set in lower-case, and in line 6 of the second stanza the misprinted word "new" has been corrected to read "now." A small hand has been printed at the beginning of the first line and the author's name is given as: "Francis S. Key, Esq. of Georgetown, District of Columbia." (See: plate 4.) This is probably the first appearance of Key's name under the heading: "Defence of Fort McHenry." This rare broadside was undoubtedly printed from the original broadside, since line 3 of the third stanza: "shall leave us no more" is the same in the two; whereas the original manuscript, the *Baltimore Patriot,* the *Baltimore American* and the *Analectic Magazine* all give: "should leave us no more." It may antedate the Carr edition and certainly could not have been copied from it since in the latter Key's name is given as "B. Key" and the title as "The Star Spangled Banner."

Another early broadside in the writer's collection which has survived the ravages of time is headed: "The Star Spangled Banner" "(Second Edition) as Sung by Miss Julia Price at the New Grotto Concert Saloon N.W. cor. of Fifth and Chesnut (!) Streets [Philadelphia]." The expression "second edition" is puzzling. It may possibly refer to an undiscovered Key manuscript in which line 3 of the third stanza reads: "they'd leave us no more," since it is thus given here. This version of the line was first used by Joseph F. Atwill, the New York publishers, in 1843.

One more interesting broadside in the writer's possession was issued in about 1861 (see: plate 5). It is printed in red and blue and gives a German translation of the song side by side with the English version. Niklas Müller of New York, is the translator and printer.

[25]

THE STAR SPANGLED BANNER. ENGLISH AND GERMAN TEXTS
Ca. 1861.

by two Baltimore newspapers and, on September 27 (1814), by the Washington *National Intelligencer.* Before the end of the year it had appeared in the *National Songster,* Hagerstown, Md. and in the *American Muse,* New York. The November number of the *Analectic Magazine* in Philadelphia, its first appearance in magazine form, printed the poem with these prophetic words: "These lines have been already published in several newspapers; they may still, however, be new to many readers. Besides we think that their merit entitles them to preservation in some more permanent form than the columns of a daily paper."

All these newspapers, book and magazine appearances of the poem omit the author's name and describe the piece as "a new song by a Gentleman of Maryland," giving the heading as: "Defence of Fort M'Henry." [8] The title: "The Star Spangled Banner" appears for the first time on a sheet-song publication arranged by Thomas Carr and printed and sold in Baltimore at "Carrs Music Store, 36 Baltimore Street" in 1814. [9]

4

Sonneck, at the time he was writing his *The Star Spangled Banner,* was unaware of the circumstances of the anthem's original arrangement and publication since the song had not been copyrighted or deposited in the Library of Congress or in the new district court of Maryland. Neither did he know of the number of sheet-music publications of the song which in the course of time were copied from the original edition as arranged and issued by the Carrs; nor of any of the other arrangements by different musicians published over a period of years. Lack of this information led him to state: . . . "no publication of 'The Star-Spangled Banner' appears among the songs deposited for copyright in the several district courts during the years 1819 to 1844 and preserved at the Library of Congress." While the book was in the hands of the printer, however, he came across two early editions of the song and amplified this statement. (Sonneck Bib. Nos. 3 and 8).

Mr. Oliver Strunk of the Library of Congress has drawn the writer's attention to an article, " 'The Star-Spangled Banner': Yesterday and To-day," published in *Musical America* for July 6, 1918, which probably is the earliest mention of the Carrs' first issue of "The Star Spangled Banner." The copy which is reproduced in facsimile was then and still is the property of Mr. W. Ward Beam, of 5021 Springfield Avenue, Philadelphia. It is dated in contemporary handwriting in "1830," a fact which

---

[8] A curious use of the heading "Defence of Fort McHenry" was made in the "National Jubilee, published annually, No. 1, New York, July 4, 1844; Wilson & Co., 162 Nassau Street." Here, Carr's version is reprinted with the title "The Star Spangled Banner; the words by Dr. McHenry," in all probability the words "Fort McHenry" in the early title had been mistaken for the author's name.

[9] Probably the first songster to print Key's lines with the title was the *American patriotic and comic modern songs,* Newburyport, 1814. Here, on page 36 and 37, the title is given: "The Star-spangled Banner; or, The Defence of Fort McHenry." Other songsters followed suit. In *The Star Spangled Banner,* Wilmington, 1816, there is no title given at beginning of the text, but in the index the song is listed as "Star spangled banner." The *New American Songster,* Philadelphia, 1817, and *The American Star,* Second Edition, Richmond, 1817, both print the title "The Star Spangled Banner" over the poem. The last named songster, which carries an engraving picturing the "Bombardment of Fort McHenry" as frontispiece, is probably the first song-book to give the author's name.

made the writer of the article, Thomas Clifford Hill, overlook the historical significance of this precious sheet-song publication.

The enviable credit for discovering its importance and for giving the first printing of our national anthem in sheet-music form its proper place in American music bibliography goes to Virginia Larkin Redway, of Ossining, N. Y.

Mrs. Redway, prior to her writing *The Carrs, American Music Publishers,* a splendid article published in the January 1931 number of *The Musical Quarterly,* came across that rare and precious Carr imprint at the Maryland Historical Society in Baltimore. Following this important find a lucky coincidence made her acquainted with the M. B. Knowles family of Yardley, Pa., the direct descendants of Thomas Carr, and among the family papers she made other invaluable discoveries.

The writer has since also had access to the Knowles collection and was able to uncover data and material concerning "The Star Spangled Banner" which made this bibliography possible.

According to members of the Knowles family the Carr manuscript of the anthem, which was written in one of his work-books along with other arrangements of songs, was in the hands of the family until a few years ago when it mysteriously disappeared.

There were two printings of the first sheet-music edition of "The Star Spangled Banner," arranged by Thomas Carr and published from the Baltimore music store. The earlier printing is made conspicuous by the misprint in the title: "pariotic" for "patriotic." In all probability this edition appeared in circulation not later than October 19th, 1814 (Bib.: No. 1).

The amended edition presumably was printed shortly after this mistake was discovered. The same plates were used except for the amended title, which spells the word "patriotic" correctly but gives the dates of the bombardment as the "12th" and "13th" of September, 1814 instead of the "13th" and "14th." Here is perhaps the first appearance of the author's name in print, but it is wrongly given as "B. Key."

In 1821 Thomas Carr published a "New Edition" from his music store at No. 78½ Baltimore Street, Baltimore. In this issue, which was newly engraved, the faulty date of the bombardment and the wrong initial in Key's name are still present.

The Carrs did not copyright their publications of "The Star Spangled Banner," but claimed their rights of authorship in notations which are printed on the bottom of page [2] in all three issues. Nevertheless, in the course of time, a number of publishers copied and reprinted Carr's versions of the song without giving him credit.

These "Carr-type" editions appeared over a period of about thirty-five years. There are eighteen on record and doubtless others were issued.[10] The earliest issue was brought out between 1814 and 1816 by A. Bacon & Co. of Philadelphia; the latest, with the New York imprint of William Hall & Son, was put into circulation in 1851. Another issue appeared with a Philadelphia imprint. This was published not before 1843—most probably before 1851—but not later than 1854. (See No. 14). No publication other than the Carr-type issues appeared until the firm of Firth & Hall of

---

[10] An edition of "The Star-spangled banner" in vocal form is advertised in a 16 page "Catalogue of vocal and instrumental music published and for sale by George Willig, No. 171 Chesnut Street, Philadelphia," 1840: a copy of which is in the Library of Congress. Willig's catalogue of 1838 does not list this publication.

[28]

New York published their edition of the song, arranged by a contemporary musician, some time between 1832 and 1839.

After this time other arrangements came along steadily and by 1861 "The Star-Spangled Banner" took the front rank among our national songs. At the beginning of the Civil War, North and South both claimed it as their own.

An edition is supposed to have been printed in New Orleans in 1858 by P. P. Werlein & Co., but no copy of this has been found.[11]

A four verse poem in imitation of Key's lines by a Southern patriot, St. George Tucker:

> "Oh, say, can you see through the gloom and the storm,
> More bright for the darkness that bright constellation . . ."

was published in 1861 in Baltimore, by Henry McCaffrey and in New Orleans by Blackmar with two separate musical settings: one called "The Southern Cross," by James Ellerbrook, the other called "The Cross of the South," by A. E. Blackmar. In 1863 the Tucker version appeared once more as "The Southern Cross" with music composed by C. L. Peticolas, a Confederate band-master.

In the North, Edna Dean Proctor, a song-writer who tried her skill at recasting various national songs to fit the spirit of the time, revised Key's lines to the original tune. Her poem, which appeared in "songsters" of the period under the titles of "The Star-Spangled Banner" and "The Stripes and the Stars," was published in sheet-music form in 1861 under the latter title by the music house of S. Brainard & Co. in Cleveland. Somewhat later in the same year, the Chicago music publisher, Higgins, re-issued the Proctor version with a new musical setting by J. P. Webster, under the title "New Star-Spangled Banner." Like hundreds of other patriotic songs this rearrangement is completely forgotten.

Several issues of "The Star Spangled Banner" were brought out in the Middle West, among them one by this same Chicago publisher Higgins. No copy of this has been found but the writer possesses another sheet-song from the series in which it was issued, where, on a collective title-page, it is advertised as follows: "H. M. Higgins' Choice Selection of Popular Songs." There were twenty-six numbers in this series, bearing the copyright notice of Higgins Bros. and the year 1857 as date of deposit.

It is curious to note that no copy of the song has been reported as issued in California where it must have been carried during the gold rush.

A curious and entertaining version of "The Star Spangled Banner," expressing sentiments which might have staggered the members of the old Anacreontic society, emanated from the brain of an ardent contributor to the *Temperance Annual and*

---

[11] The firm of P. P. Werlein & Co., who printed the first (pirated) edition of Daniel Decatur Emmet's "Dixie," was one of the leading southern music publishing concerns. In 1865, when New Orleans was under occupation of Federal forces, all music publishing in that city was greatly interfered with. General Butts, the commander, fined some of the music stores for printing and selling southern patriotic songs and ordered his troops to confiscate and destroy all the plates and music they could lay their hands on. Southern imprints are accordingly extremely scarce.

THE STAR SPANGLED BANNER
Parody Published in the *Temperance Annual and Cold Water Magazine*, 1843.

Cold Water Magazine, Vol. 1, No. 4, 1843 (see: plate 6). Another parody of the song in celebration of prohibition,

> "Oh, say can you see by the dawn's early light,
> That intemp'rance, ever firmly entrenched, is awaning . .."

appeared in 1888 in *The Temperance Rallying Songs,* written and published by Asa Hull.

An obvious parody of both words and music of "The Star Spangled Banner," used for the same cause, was published in 1853 by Firth, Pond & Co. in a set of six songs performed by the Alleghanians, a traveling troupe of entertainers. This "The Appeal of the Reformed Inebriate" was written by Mrs. Ellen Stone and set to music by Joseph P. Webster (1820–1875), a popular song writer of his day, best remembered by "Lorena," "Sweet By and By" and "The Golden Stair." The first of four stanzas reads:

> "Oh call us not back to the festival board,
> To the gay lighted hall, where the wine cup is poured,
> We come not, we heed not, from fountain and rill
> We fill up the goblet, and drink to you still.
>
> Chorus.
> We drink to the hour when like us you shall be,
> With the heart of the brave in the home of the free;
> We drink to the hour when our banner shall wave
> O'er the land of the free and the home of the brave!"

The poetess who patterned her lines after Key, apparently meant this "paen" to be sung to the tune of "The Star Spangled Banner." Instead of it, Webster, a song writer of reputation, borrowed some musical phrases of the "Anacreontic Song" and concocted a poor substitute devoid of all musical inspiration.

After the beginning of the Civil War, "The Star-Spangled Banner" was played throughout the North by military bands and orchestras, sung in theatres and in the homes of the people and included in every kind of a song-book. Numerous editions of it appeared in vocal and instrumental music-sheet form. Among the latter were several publications which included an extra stanza by Oliver Wendell Holmes written in indignation when the flag was fired on at Fort Sumter.[12]

5

In spite of its popularity among the people, Key's song has been over a hundred years in winning official acceptance. Critics have attacked the tune both because it is borrowed and because, with its awkward range of melody, it is hard to sing. They have objected to the peculiar meter of the poem which makes the words difficult to memo-

---

[12] The writer will consider this stanza in the bibliography of the various editions of the poem.

THE PILLAR OF GLORY
Published in the *Port Folio,* November 1813.

1.

HAIL to the Heroes whose triumphs have brighten'd
    The darkness which shrouded America's name;
Long shall their valor in battle that lighten'd,
    Live in the brilliant escutcheons of fame:
        Dark where the torrents flow,
        And the rude tempests blow,
The stormy clad Spirit of Albion raves;
        Long shall she mourn the day,
        When, in the vengeful fray,
Liberty walk'd like a God on the waves.

2.

The ocean, ye cheifs, (the region of glory,
    Where Fortune has destin'd Columbia to reign,)
Gleams with the hale and lustre of story,
    That curl round the wave as the scene of her fame:
        There, on its raging tide,
        Shall her proud Navy ride,
The bulwark of freedom, protected by Heav'n;
        There shall her haughty foe,
        Bow to her prowess low,
There shall renown to her heroes be giv'n.

3.

The Pillar of Glory, the sea that enlightens
    Shall last till Eternity rocks on its base,
The splendor of Fame its waters that brightens,
    Shall light the footsteps of Time in his race:
        Wide o'er the stormy deep,
        Where the rude surges sweep,
Its lustre shall circle the brows of the brave;
        Honor shall give it light,
        Triumph shall keep it bright,
Long as in battle we meet on the wave.

4.

Already the storm of contention has hurl'd,
    From the grasp of Old England the *Trident of War*,
The beams of our *Stars* have illumin'd the world,
    Unfurl'd our Standard beats proud in the air:
        Wild glares the Eagle's eye,
        Swift as he cuts the sky,
Marking the wake where our heroes advance;
        Compass'd with rays of light,
        Hovers he o'er the fight;
Albion is heartless—and stoops to his glance.

THE PILLAR OF GLORY
Published in the *Port Folio,* November 1813.

rize. The sentiments of its words have been branded foreign to genuine Americanism. For all of that "The Star-Spangled Banner" is the most stirring of national patriotic airs. It is not written, like the national hymns of England and Austria, for the glorification and flattery of a ruler, nor, like the "Marseillaise," as a call to arms; it celebrates the preservation of the flag, it is the symbol of liberty, law and order. Flag and song belong together.

The search for an appropriate American national ode has been going on for more than a century. National institutions, private individuals, even the government itself have fostered prize contests in which participants have been called on to contribute suitable words and music (original or adapted) for a national hymn. As early as 1806 the "Militia Military Association of Philadelphia" offered a gold medal of the value of fifty dollars for the best "national song or martial tune." The prize went to A. Wilson for a ten stanza poem entitled: "Freedom and Peace; American National Martial Song":

"While Europe's mad Pow'rs o'er the ocean are ranging
Regardless of right, with their blood-hounds of war . . ."

This lyrical outburst, which fortunately is forgotten today, was adapted to a march by Raynor Taylor, one of Philadelphia's most eminent musicians.

The *Port Folio,* a monthly magazine conducted by "Oliver Oldschool, Esq." in Philadelphia, frequently offered premiums for patriotic songs. In November 1813, two one-hundred dollar prizes for "the best two Naval songs" were awarded. The first prize went to Edwin C. Holland, of Charleston, S. C. for his poem "The Pillar of Glory, A Naval Song" which appeared as a supplement to the *Port Folio.* The same number carried, as a second supplement, a naval song by the same author, "Rise Columbia, Brave and True," which, in the editor's words, "is less striking in its effect, but being too valuable to be overlooked, is presented to the public, who will appreciate its value." Both poems were set to "original and appropriate music composed for the occasion" by Jacob Eckhard, Senior, Organist of St. Michael's Church. Comparison of the Charleston organist's musical setting of Holland's "The Pillar of Glory" with the music of the early "Adams and Liberty" (1798) shows plainly that the melodic construction is patterned after the tune "To Anacreon in Heaven." Both songs are in the key of C major and, with due allowance for the differences in their meters, their melodies are strikingly similar. (See: plates 7 and 7a).

It is highly probable that Key was familiar with the wording of these and other patriotic outpourings of the time and unconsciously followed their general pattern. Such phrases as: "Unfurl'd our Standard beats proud in the air," "The Stars that in thy Banner shine," and "Its Stripes shall awe the vassal deep" are very reminiscent of the predecessor of "The Star Spangled Banner."

A few months before Key wrote his lines, the *Port Folio,* in its number for May, 1814, once again offered a premium of fifty dollars for the best national song to be submitted by the fifteenth day of June, 1814 and serve for the Fourth of July celebration. None of the twelve contestants, however, was considered worthy of the trophy. The choice of the judges was printed in the July number under the heading:

[34]

"The Birth-day of Freedom."

("All hail to the Birth of the happiest Land
That the Sun in his journey is proud to awaken. . .")

a poem of eight verses which was reprinted and was to be sung to the tune of "To Anacreon in Heaven."

In 1816 James Hewitt, an early American musician, composer and music publisher, wishing to replace the old English drinking song with native music, wrote an original tune for Key's "The Star Spangled Banner." This effort was musically of little importance, since the tune is by no means an improvement over the English air. It is even more difficult to sing than the "Anacreon" melody, ranging from D to high G, and unlike the English tune, it is lacking in musical inspiration. That it enjoyed popularity for some time is evident from the number of editions that came into circulation. Hewitt himself first published his "The Star Spangled Banner" from his "Musical Repository" at No. 156½ William Street, New York, in 1819. This date has been established by a copyright deposit in the Library of Congress of "This Blooming Rose at Early Dawn," a song by T. Philips, and issued by Hewitt and deposited for copyright May 20, 1819. The publisher was listed in New York directories as "musician" at No. 20 Harrison Street in 1818, and at No. 87 Warren Street in 1819. These two addresses were most probably Hewitt's home addresses. 156½ William Street was his place of business for that period. Hewitt disappears from city records after 1819, and went to live in Boston. In 1820 or 1821, J. A. & W. Geib of New York apparently acquired the plates of this song from Hewitt, and republished it, with their imprint. In 1829 it was reissued with the imprint of Geib & Walker. Between 1819 and 1831 another New York publisher, E. Riley, at No. 29 Chatham Street, brought out a new edition without Hewitt's name. The song finally died a natural and deserved death. Numerous other attempts to supplant Key's anthem over a period of years failed similarly.

In the fifties, P. T. Barnum, that prince of advertisers, instituted a prize contest for the "best national song," but the prize-money remained unpaid for lack of a genius who could write a made-to-order national ode.

An entertaining account of another prize competition promoted by a group of patriotically-minded citizens in New York in June, 1861, is given by Richard Grant White in his book *National Hymns,* (New York, 1861). In the author's words·

"A vast washing-basket—a 'buck-basket,' big enough to hold Falstaff himself—was made the temporary tomb of these extinguished hopes; and this receptacle was filled five times with rejected manuscripts, which were seized upon for incendiary purposes by the cooks of the gentlemen at whose houses the meetings of the committee took place. . . . The mass of these manuscripts were 'only of interest to their writers' or, in plain terms, either the flattest commonplace, or absolutely neither rhyme nor reason. From the whole collection only about thirty were reserved as worthy of a second read-

[35]

ing, and these, on second and third examination, were reduced about one half. . . ."

No award was made. A few of the twelve hundred compositions submitted were reprinted as notable for poetic excellence, among them "E Pluribus Unum," a four stanza poem by the Rev. John Pierpont, to be sung to the air of "The Star-Spangled Banner."

As recently as July, 1928 a national anthem contest with a three-thousand dollar main prize was announced in New York City under the sponsorship of Mrs. Florence Brooks-Aten. Four-thousand-five-hundred manuscripts were submitted, according to newspaper reports, but no final decision was reached.

These are but a few of the many attempts that have been made to call into being a national anthem to take the place of the existing national songs.

Meanwhile Key's lines to the Anacreontic tune have come to be thought of by the great majority of the people as the national anthem. When the song first appeared, it gained immediate popularity in Baltimore and was widely sung in the camps around the city. In the Civil War, the Spanish-American War and the World War it held first place in the ranks of national songs. It was the favorite song of the A. E. F. At last Congress enacted a law declaring "The Star-Spangled Banner" the national anthem of the United States of America. To add a humorous touch, various ardent prohibitionists protested against the official adoption of a tune which had been written as a drinking song, but in spite of these objections, on March 3, 1931, President Hoover signed the necessary document and, after a delay of one hundred and seventeen years, the people's choice among American patriotic songs became part of the law of the land. (See: plate 8).

Seventy-first Congress of the United States of America;

At the Third Session,

Begun and held at the City of Washington on Monday, the first
day of December, one thousand nine hundred and thirty.

AN ACT

To make The Star-Spangled Banner the national anthem of the
United States of America.

*Be it enacted by the Senate and House of Representatives of the
United States of America in Congress assembled*, That the composi-
tion consisting of the words and music known as The Star-Spangled
Banner is designated the national anthem of the United States of
America.

Nicholas Longworth

Speaker of the House of Representatives.

Charles Curtis

*Vice President of the United States and
President of the Senate.*

Approved, March 3, 1931,

Herbert Hoover,

FACSIMILE OF ORIGINAL BILL DECLARING "THE STAR SPANGLED BANNER"
THE NATIONAL ANTHEM

A

CATALOGUE

OF THE VALUABLE

STOCK in TRADE,

OF

Mr. Joseph Carr,

Of MIDDLE ROW, HOLBORN,

MUSIC SELLER,

QUITTING BUSINESS.

CONSISTING OF

A Variety of Harpſichords, Grand Piano-Fortes, Organs, Guitars, and Dulcimers, Twiſting Machines, and Working Tools; an Aſſortment of Printed Muſic, by the beſt Compoſers, Copper Plates, &c.

TOGETHER

With the Remaining HOUSEHOLD FURNITURE, Books, an Eight-day Clock, and other Effects,

WHICH WILL BE SOLD BY AUCTION,

By Mr. WEALE,

ON THE PREMISES,

On FRIDAY, the 14th of FEBRUARY, 1794, Preciſely at Twelve o'Clock.

———

To be Viewed on Thurſday preceding the Sale.

Catalogues may be had on the Premiſes; at Garraway's Coffee-Houſe; and of Mr. WEALE, Sworn Exchange Broker, Caſtle Street, Holborn.

TITLE-PAGE OF JOSEPH CARR'S SALE CATALOGUE, LONDON, FEBRUARY 14, 1794
From the Knowles Collection.

THE CARRS

The Carr family of pioneer music publishers came to this country from England at the close of the eighteenth century. Joseph Carr, the head of the family, had been engaged in the music trade in London. In the writer's collection are a number of vocal pieces bearing the notation: "Printed for J. Carr, Middle Row, Holborn." His elder son Benjamin was the first of the family to come across the water and set up shop at No. 136 High Street, Philadelphia, under the firm name of B. Carr and Co., apparently in anticipation of the arrival of his family.[13] The father with his wife and son Thomas—whose name was to be so intimately associated with the original publication of the national anthem—seems to have arrived in the spring or early summer of 1794 (see: Sale Catalogue from the Knowles collection: plate 9), remained temporarily with Benjamin, and in the summer opened a music store in Baltimore.

For a while after his family had left him Benjamin maintained a branch store in New York at 131 William Street. Late in 1797 he sold this business to his friend and fellow musician, James Hewitt, and made Philadelphia his permanent home.

Benjamin Carr was the most famous and versatile member of the Carr family. For a time he appeared with moderate success as a ballad singer and actor on the operatic stage; but he soon earned for himself an important position in Philadelphia musical life and wide cultural influence throughout the Republic as organist, pianist, composer and music publisher.

Meanwhile Joseph Carr had set up his "Musical Repository" on Market (also called Baltimore) Street, near Gay Street, Baltimore,[14] and on August 6, 1794 the following notice appeared in the *Maryland Journal*:

---

[13] According to Sonneck in his Bibliography, *Early Secular American Music*: "Benjamin Carr emigrated to New York early in 1793, when he immediately began his career as music dealer and publisher at 131 William st. Shortly afterwards in the same year the firm of 'B. Carr & Co., music printers and importers' was founded in Philadelphia and existed until fall, 1794. B. Carr then carried business on alone at the Musical Repository, 122 Market st."

Available records, however, partially contradict this statement. Benjamin is not listed in New York city directories for 1793, and no newspaper announcements of his publications have been found that early. Sonneck records that "Freedom triumphant a new song" is advertised by B. Carr, No. 131 William Street, New York, in April, 1793, as just published. He also lists, however: "Call Freedom triumphant, New Song" advertised by the same firm in April, 1796. The most plausible hypothesis is that these two songs are one and the same, and that the date 1793 in the former advertisement is a misprint for 1796. Not until 1795 is Carr listed as "Benjamin Carr, music and musical instrument seller, 137 William St." (apparently a typographic error for 131 William St.) nor can imprints with his New York address be traced. Moreover he is first listed in Philadelphia city directories in 1794 as "Benjamin Carr, musical repository, 122 High Street (also known as Market Street) and never as "B. Carr & Co."

The original firm of B. Carr & Co., which existed for a little over a year according to the evidence of imprints and newspaper announcements, issued a great deal of music between August, 1793 and July, 1794. Sonneck lists a number of pieces, giving the advertised publication dates where he had not seen the actual imprints. Since then, however, a number of these publications have come to light.

[14] From 1795 to 1802 Carr was at No. 6 North Gay Street. For the next two years his music

JOSEPH CARR
From the Portrait in the Knowles Collection.

"J. Carr, Music Importer, lately from London, Respectfully informs the public that he has opened a Store entirely in the Musical line, and has for sale, Finger and barrel organs, double and single key'd harpsichords; piano fortes and common guitars."

By the fall of 1794 the Carr family was thus well established in three large American cities: Joseph and his younger son Thomas in Baltimore, and Benjamin in New York and Philadelphia.

Joseph and Thomas were both able musicians and much in demand in Baltimore. For years the father was organist at the old St. Paul's Church, while the son filled the same post at Christ Church, a branch of St. Paul's located in the same parish. Thomas also was known as a composer and had some reputation for his clever musical arrangements of songs.

In February, 1806, Thomas, at the age of twenty-six, married Milcah Merryman, the daughter of a prominent Baltimore County family and in the course of years became the father of five daughters and seven sons. Portraits of the couple painted in water-colors on silk, presumably at the time of their marriage, are treasured heirlooms in the Knowles collection. Thomas appears as a debonair young blade with brown eyes and curly chestnut hair.

On September 20, 1819, Joseph Carr, feeling that death was near, made his will. The deed, duly signed and witnessed, called for the payment of five dollars current from son to father, after which formality Thomas was declared sole heir of the estate. The only stipulation in the indenture was that Thomas "twelve months after the decease of the said Joseph Carr pay to his son Benjamin Carr of Philadelphia the sum of one hundred Dollars." A notation in the family bible soon after records: "Joseph Carr (consort of Mary) died on the twenty-seventh day of October, one thousand eight hundred and nineteen in the eightieth year of his age."

Thus Thomas became the owner of the flourishing music store and publishing house, then located at No. 36 Baltimore Street, where the words of our national anthem were first set to music and printed. The house is still standing. It is now No. 616 East Baltimore Street and the premises are occupied by the Home Lighting Co. The site of the building, which in all these years has doubtless passed through various stages of remodeling and renovation, has been positively verified by Mr. Louis H. Dielman, the librarian of the Maryland Historical Society, Baltimore. A movement is in progress to mark the structure with a bronze plate in commemoration of the birth of "The Star-Spangled Banner" in musical form.

---

and instrument store was situated at the "corner of Baltimore and N. Gay St." and "Baltimore cross N. Gay St."—probably one and the same address. Although the city directories fail to list his name chronologically, he appears in 1807 at No. 48 Baltimore St. and in 1810 at the "north west corner Baltimore and Gay St." From 1814 to 1819 he is listed at No. 36 Baltimore St.

The writer owns a vocal piece imprinted: "The young May Moon-Baltimore, Printed and Sold at Carrs Music Store, 109½ Baltimore Street" which ought to stimulate bibliographical research. There is no such address on record, but the type-setting and lettering of the publisher's imprint line is very similar to that used by the Carrs between 1814 and 1819. It may therefore belong to the period of their activities between 1810 and 1813. A search through the files of contemporary Baltimore newspapers might confirm this supposition.

After his father's death Thomas Carr's business did not seem to thrive. Before the end of the year he had moved to No. 78½ Baltimore Street where, according to an advertisement on June 14, 1820, he had a "stock of 2,000 plates daily augmenting," but shortly after this he opened a "Musical Academy" at No. 20 North Gay Street and late in 1822 or early in 1823 he gave up the business altogether, sold out and went to live in Philadelphia. His stock and catalogue were acquired by George Willig, Jr. and John Cole, both Baltimore publishers who were just entering business.

Thomas Carr is listed in Philadelphia city directories at various street addresses as: "professor and vendor of music." A number of publications exist which bear his Philadelphia imprint, proving that he continued to publish music as well. Among these issues are "Home, Sweet Home" and "Welcome Fayette, composed in honour of that illustrious general by Joseph Taw," both imprinted: "Philadelphia, Printed for the Composer & Sold at T. Carr's Musical Academy No. 132 South Second Street [his residential address from 1824 to 1827]." Other imprints bear the address No. 58 South Fourth Street, where he is never listed in the directories.

In his later years Thomas became a staunch partisan of the Whig cause. In 1840 he wrote and also arranged several songs in support of General Harrison. Two of the outstanding ones are: "Old Tippecanoe's Raisin," ("Come all you Log Cabin boys, we're going to have a raisin . . ."), "sung with volcanic effect by the Buckeye Blacksmith, dedicated to the friends of Liberty and Reform"; and "Turn Out! To the Rescue!" ("In 'Old Kentuck' the People say, That Matty Van has had his day . . .") [15]

Carr died on April 15, 1849, by a striking coincidence, at the exact moment as his wife Milcah.

Among the Carr family papers preserved in the Knowles collection are some excerpts from the correspondence of Mary Jordan Carr Merryman, the daughter of Thomas Carr, with James Warrington, the hymnologist of 303 Walnut Street, Philadelphia, who, as far as we know, never made any use of them. They relate mainly to an article which aroused her ire: "The Star-Spangled Banner" written by John C. Carpenter and published in the number of the *Century Illustrated Monthly Magazine* for July, 1894. Like all other published accounts of the song it did not credit her father either with having originally arranged the anthem or with having published it from her grandfather's place of business. In one of the notes reproduced she says in rather awkwardly chosen words:

---

[15] The tune of "To Anacreon in Heaven" and its most famous offspring was much in evidence during the Harrison campaign. Tippecanoe song-books contain numerous rallying-songs written to this air. One of these campaign-songs, "The Whigs of Columbia shall surely prevail" ("Ye Whigs of Columbia whose fathers have fought . . .") appeared in broadside form with the musical setting of "To Anacreon in Heaven." It is embellished at the top with a cut showing a log cabin and a large flowing American flag bearing the inscription: "Harrison and Reform." No publisher's name is given. This same parody was published in sheet-music form by the Providence firm of Oliver Shaw in 1840. Its musical arrangement, for voice and a chorus for three voices with piano accompaniment, however, is the Carr version of "The Star Spangled Banner."

[42]

THOMAS CARR
From the Portrait in the Knowles Collection.

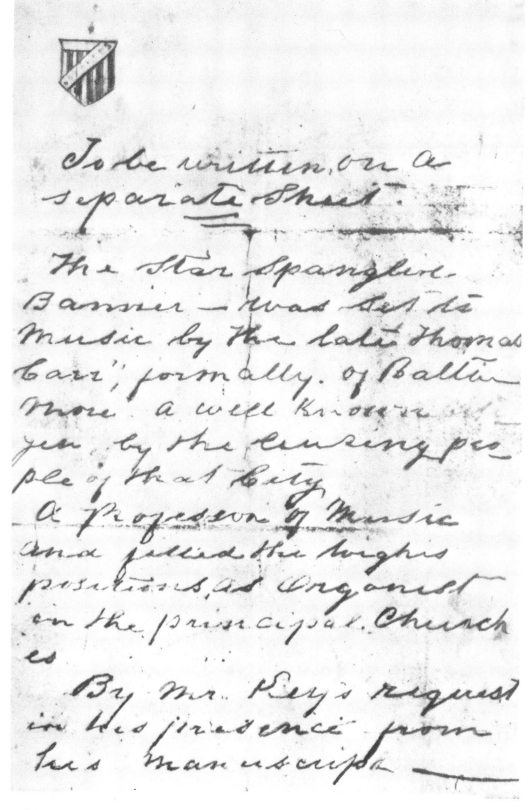

To be written, on a
separate Sheet.

The Star Spangled
Banner — was Set to
Music by the late Thomas
Carr", formally. of Baltimore. a well known
yet, by the ensuing peo-
ple of that City.
a Professor of Music
and filled the highes
positions, as Organist
in the principal. Church
es

By mr. Key's request
in his presence from
his manuscript ——

EXCERPTS FROM THE CORRESPONDENCE OF MARY JORDAN CARR
From the Knowles Collection.

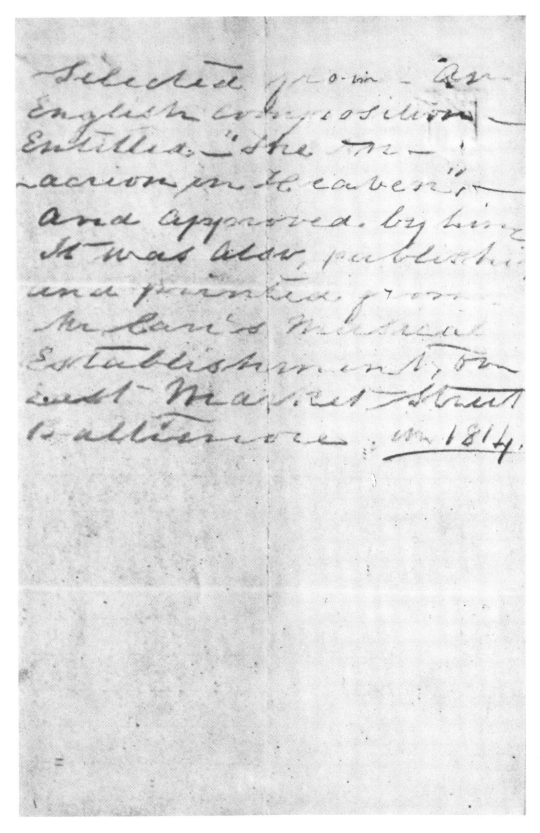

EXCERPTS FROM THE CORRESPONDENCE OF MARY JORDAN CARR
From the Knowles Collection.

"The Star Spangled Banner—was set to Music by the late Thomas Carr, formerly of Baltimore—a well known citizen by the leading people of that City.

"A Professor of Music—and filled the highest positions as Organist in the principal Churches.

By Mr. Key's request in his presence from his manuscript selected from an English Composition—Entitled "The Anacreon in Heaven"—and approved by him.

"It was also published and printed from Mr. Carr's Musical Establishment in East Market Street Baltimore in 1814." (See: plates 12 and 12a).

Note to frontispiece portrait

The frontispiece portrait is that of Francis Scott Key, said to have been made "just prior to writing of 'Star Spangled Banner'," and to have been in the possession of Key until his death in January 1843. The cut was made from a photograph taken of the painting by Kurtz, the New York photographer, for the *Century Illustrated Monthly Magazine* where it appeared as a wood engraving by T. Johnson in the July 1894 number with the article "The Star Spangled Banner" by John C. Carpenter. The painting, which is owned by Key's great-grandson, Mr. Cooper Hunt Pendleton, of 7 East Eighty-sixth Street, New York City, has recently been reproduced in newspapers. Comparison of these cuts with the photograph here reproduced show that the painting, which has been renovated since then, has suffered the loss of some of its former excellence.

BIBLIOGRAPHY

AUTHOR'S NOTE

In a work of this kind it is necessary to choose some form of arbitrary order for the items listed, which, by the very fact that it is arbitrary, fails to provide for special cases, and causes the grouping sometimes to seem rather indiscriminate. The writer has chosen the chronological order for this bibliography, hoping that strict adherence to it will provide the maximum of clarity which is the first duty of a reference-book.

No separate title-page.

THE | STAR SPANGLED BANNER | A PARIOTIC SONG. |

Baltimore. Printed and sold at CARRS Music Store 36 Baltimore Street. | Air. Anacreon in Heaven.

————————

No date.

This publication is the original edition of "The Star Spangled Banner" set to music.

Music and text fill two unpaged inside pages.

The principal identification mark of this edition is the absence of the first letter "t" in the word "Patriotic" in the title.

In the lower margins of both pages appears the notation: "(Adap'd & Arr'd by T.C.)," and the marks "(Pl.1)" and "Pl.2)" respectively. The lower margins of pages [1] and [2] bear the code "(T.s.s.b.)"

The music is an arrangement for voice and piano accompaniment in 6/4 time in the key of C major, followed with the air for the flute in D. It is adapted to "The Anacreontic Song as Sung at the Crown and Anchor Tavern in the Strand—the Words by Ralph Tomlinson Esqr. late President of the Society. (London) Printed by Longman & Broderip No. 26 Cheapside." (See: Sonneck, *The Star Spangled Banner;* plate VIII.)

In the text the latter half of line 3 of third stanza reads: "shall leave us no more" instead of "should leave us no more," the version found in all existing copies of Key's poem in his own handwriting and in early printings of "Defence of Fort M'Henry." On the other hand, the broadside which Judge Nicholson had printed (See: Sonneck; plate XV.) uses the word "shall." Carr, no doubt used a copy of it for his publication. This variation is found in many subsequent editions of the song in sheet-music form.

The Carr family papers furnish sufficient evidence to prove that T. Carr was responsible for the first appearance in print of Key's poem under the title of "The Star Spangled Banner." The publisher, as has been mentioned in the introduction, was visited by Key and requested to put the lines to music. The result was the arrangement of the song as we have it today.

The title of the song, presumably, was agreed upon at that meeting. The exact date of their meeting or the time of year when "The Star Spangled Banner" was released for publication is not on record. It may safely be assumed that the poet made his call shortly after the memorable occurrence that inspired him to write the poem. This supposition is further strengthened by a statement of T. Carr's daughter, Mary Jordan Carr (Knowles collection) that: "It was (also) published and printed from

THE STAR SPANGLED BANNER
Published by Joseph Carr, Baltimore.
First Edition. (Bib. No. 1.)

On the shore dimly seen through the mists of the deep,
    Where the foe's haughty host in dread silence reposes,
What is that which the breeze, o'er the towering steep,
    As it fitfully blows, half conceals, half discloses;
Now it catches the gleam of the morning's first beam,
In full glory reflected now shines in the stream,
    'Tis the star spangled banner.O. long may it wave
O'er the land of the free, and the home of the brave.

(3)
And where is that band who so vauntingly swore
    That the havoc of war and the battle's confusion
A home and a country, shall leave us no more.
    Their blood has wash'd out their foul footsteps pollution.
No refuge could save the hireling and slave,
From the terror of flight or the gloom of the grave,
    And the star spangled banner, in triumph doth wave
    O'er the Land &c.

(4)
O! thus be it ever when freemen shall stand,
    Between their lov'd home, and the war's desolation,
Blest with vict'ry and peace, may the Heav'n rescued land
    Praise the Pow'r that hath made and preserv'd us a nation!
Then conquer we must, when our cause it is just,
And this be our motto—"In God is our Trust;"
    And the star spangled banner, in triumph shall wave,
    O'er the Land &c.

(Adapd. & Arrd. by T.C.)

(Pl.2.)

THE STAR SPANGLED BANNER
Published by Joseph Carr, Baltimore.
First Edition. (Bib. No. 1.)

Mr. Carr's establishment in East Market Street (No. 36 Baltimore Street; Market Street being also called Baltimore Street) in 1814."

It is not logical to assume that Key changed the name from "Defence of Fort M'Henry" to "The Star Spangled Banner," since the poem had already been published and reprinted under the original heading. The elder Carr, being a good business man, in all probability suggested the title "The Star Spangled Banner" to add national appeal. The Carrs were known as being always first to print popular patriotic music. "Hail Columbia," for example, was first published by Benjamin Carr in Philadelphia in 1798.

There has been a certain amount of confusion caused by the appearance of an undated sheet-music publication entitled "The Battle of the Wabash" together with "The Star Spangled Banner" and "To Anacreon in Heaven," and several collectors of early American music have claimed that this issue antedated the Carr issue. Careful examination of the facts as we have them entirely disproves this theory.

The original song-sheet publication "The Battle of the Wabash," one of the numerous Anacreontic offshoots, celebrates the battle of Tippecanoe, fought under the command of General William Henry Harrison, November 7, 1811. Like the majority of early music it bears neither date, plate number nor address by which the time of publication can be traced. Certainly, however, "The Battle of the Wabash" was written long before "The Star Spangled Banner" which proves beyond question that this issue containing the three songs, "The Battle of the Wabash," "The Star Spangled Banner," and "To Anacreon in Heaven," is a reprint issued indefinitely later than the original edition—which might put it at any date during the War of 1812. There is here then no respectable evidence for believing that in the case of "The Star Spangled Banner" alone the Carrs failed to be first in the field.

There is, however, one very interesting point connecting the "Battle of the Wabash" with "The Star Spangled Banner" bibliography. In this reprint is the only appearance known of the words of "The Star Spangled Banner" together with the words of "To Anacreon in Heaven."

Sonneck, in his *The Star Spangled Banner* supplies information shedding further light on this controversy. On page 77 he states that Baltimore papers announce the historical play "Count Benyowski" (by Boieldieu) for performance on Wednesday evening, October 19, 1814, and that:

"After the play, Mr. Hardinge will sing a much admired New Song written by a gentleman of Maryland, in commemoration of the GALLANT DEFENCE OF FORT M'HENRY, called, THE STAR SPANGLED BANNER . ."

It is evident from the above that the Blake music sheet was reprinted sometime after the 19th of October 1814.

His reprint has a very strange appearance. Mr. Blake, who gave his Philadelphia clients their money's worth, manipulated the original Wabash plates and, instead of

THE BATTLE OF THE WABASH
Published by G. E. Blake, Philadelphia.
Page [1]. (Bib. No. 1.)

THE BATTLE OF THE WABASH
Published by G. E. Blake, Philadelphia.
Amended Edition. Page [1]. *(Bib. No. 1.)*

The lyrics beneath the music (music staves shown above with words):
"...spice you to boot, And be sides. I'll instruct you like me to ... Twine, The slain in the fight; But the laurel shall e_ver con_ti_nue to wave; And Myrtle of Venus with Bacchus's vine, And be_sides I'll instruct_you like glory thus bloom o'er the tomb of the brave, But the laurel shall e_ver con_me to in_twine, The myrtle of Venus with Bacchus's Vine._ti_nue to wave, And glory thus bloom o'er the tomb of the brave."

Chorus

2.

Great Daviess and Owen, bright offspring of Fame,
 Rushed on to the battle, with bosoms undaunted;
And ere bearing death the dread rifle ball came
 In the breast of the foe oft their weapons they planted.
  Gallant chieftains adieu,
  Tears your destiny drew,
Yet shall rise o'er your tombs neither cypress nor yew,
 But the laurel &c.

3.

Long, Warwick, McMahon and Spencer and Baen,
 And Berry, 'mid darkness, their banners defended;
But when day drew the curtain of night they were seen,
 Covered o'er with the blood of the savage, extended!
  Though Freedom may weep,
  Where they mouldering sleep
Yet shall valour their deaths as a Jubilee keep,
 While the laurel &c.

4.

Ye chiefs of the Wabash, who gallantly fought,
 And fearlessly heard the dread storm of war rattle;
Who lived to see conquest so terribly bought,
 While your brothers were slain in the uproar of battle,
  Still fearless remain,
  And though stretched on the plain,
You shall rise on the records of Freedom again,
 For the laurel &c.

5.

Ye sons of Columbia, when danger is nigh,
 And Liberty calls round her standard to rally;
For your Country, your wives, and your children, to die,
 Resolve on your foes, in stern valour to sally;
  Every hero secure,
  That his fame shall endure,
'Till eternity, time in oblivion immure;
 For the laurel &c.

2.
The news through Olympus immediately flew,
When old Thunder pretended to give himself airs_
"If these mortals are suffer'd their scheme to persue,
"The devil a Goddess will stay above stairs.
"Hark! already they cry_In transports of joy,
"Away to the Sons of Anacreon we'll fly,
"And there with good fellows we'll learn to intwine &c.

3.
"The Yellow hair'd God and his nine fusty maids,
"From Helicon's banks will incontinent flee,
"Idalia will boast but of tenantless shades,
"And the bi_forked hill a mere desart will be,
"My thunder, no fear on't_Shall soon do its errand,
"And, damme! I'll swinge the ringleaders, I warrant,
"I'll trim the young dogs, for thus daring to twine &c.

Ye sons of Anacreon, then join hand in hand,
Preserve unanimity, friendship and love!
Tis yours to support what's so happily plann'd,
You've the sanction of Gods, and the fiat of Jove.

4.
Apollo rose up, and said, "prythee ne'er quarrel,
"Good king of the Gods, with my vot'ries below;
"Your thunder is useless_then, shewing his laurel,
Cry'd, "Sic evitabile fulmen_you know!
"Then over each head_My laurels I'll spread,
"So my sons from your crackers no mischief shall dread,
"Whilst snug in their Club-room, they jovially twine &c.

5.
Next Momus got up, with his risible phiz,
And swore with Apollo he'd chearfully join_
"The full tide of harmony still shall be his,
"But the song, and the catch, and the laugh shall be mine.
"Then, Jove be not jealous_Of these honest fellows,
Cry'd Jove, "we relent, since the truth you now tell us;
"And swear, by old Styx, that they long shall entwine &c.

While thus we agree_Our toast let it be,
May our Club flourish happy, united and free.
And long may the Sons of Anacreon entwine,
The Myrtle of Venus with Bacchus's vine.

THE BATTLE OF THE WABASH
Published by G. E. Blake, Philadelphia.
Amended Edition. Page [2]. (Bib. No. 1.)

FORT McHENRY,

OR, THE STAR SPANGLED BANNER

Sung with great applause by Mr. Hardinge, at the Theatre Baltimore.

AIR, ANACREON IN HEAVEN.

1st

O, say can you see by the dawn's early light,
 What so proudly we hail'd at the twilight's last gleaming,
Whose broad stripes and bright stars thro' the perilous fight,
 O'er the ramparts we watch'd were so gallantly streaming,
And the rockets red glare, the bombs bursting in air,
 Gave proof through the night that our flag was still there.
O! say does that star spangled banner yet wave,
 O'er the land of the free, and the home of the brave.

2nd

On the shore dimly seen thro' the mists of the deep,
 Where the foe's haughty host in dread silence reposes;
What is that which the breeze, o'er the towering steep,
 As it fitfully blows, half conceals, half discloses;
Now it catches the gleam of the morning's first beam,
 In full glory reflected new shines in the stream:
Tis the star spangled banner, O! long may it wave,
 O'er the land of the free, and the home of the brave.

3rd

And where is that band who so vauntingly swore,
 That the havoc of war and the battle's confusion,
A home and a country, shall leave us no more
 Their blood has wash'd out their foul footsteps pollution
No refuge could save the hireling and slave,
 From the terror of flight or the gloom of the grave:
And the star spangled banner in triumph doth wave,
 O'er the land of the free and the home of the brave.

4th

O! thus be it ever, when freemen shall stand
 Between their lov'd home, and the war's disolation,
Blest with vict'ry and peace, may the heav'n rescued land
 Praise the pow'r that hath made and preserv'd us a nation:
Then conquer we must, when our cause it is just,
 And this be our motto—"in god is our trust,"
And the star spangled banner in triumph shall wave,
 O'er the land of the free, and the home of the brave!

THE BATTLE OF THE WABASH
Published by G. E. Blake, Philadelphia.
Amended Edition. Page [3]. *(Bib. No. 1.)*

printing it on two inside pages, he used the front and back of a single sheet, which not only contains the original Wabash song but the first verse of the old "Anacreontic ode" interlineated with the Wabash words. On the back of the page the remaining five stanzas of "To Anacreon in Heaven" are crammed in under the Wabash poem, and on a separate blank sheet Key's poem is printed, broadside fashion, under the caption:

"FORT Mc.HENRY, | or, THE STAR SPANGLED BANNER. | Sung with great applause by Mr. Hardinge, at the Theatre Baltimore. | AIR. ANACREON IN HEAVEN."

Hardinge, whose name appears on several earlier patriotic songs published by Blake, seems to have been the latter's "song-plugger." Probably the singer came across the Carr publication when he was engaged in Baltimore or Carr, himself, may have shown it to him. Meanwhile Blake, getting news of the successful performance of the new patriotic song and already having a music-sheet publication to the tune of "To Anacreon in Heaven," copied the words either from the Carr edition or from the broadside appearance of the poem and issued his edition. The slip-shod manner in which the music-sheet was printed makes one guess that it was thrown together under great pressure for time.

The Carr and Blake versions of the poem are practically the same except for a few differences in punctuation and abbreviation. Both of them are copied from the original broadside (see: Sonneck; plate XV) and not from the other contemporary printings of "Defence of Fort M'Henry." (See: Sonneck; plates XIII; XIV and XVI.)

The following are the variations adopted by all three copies: (the handbill and the two music-sheet issues.) Line 6 of second stanza reads "reflected 'new' shines in the stream" instead of "reflected 'now' shines in the stream, and line 3 of third stanza reads "A home and a country 'shall' leave us no more" instead of "A home and a country 'should' leave us no more."

A more careful comparison discloses a few slight additional differences in Blake's imprint. These occur in the fourth stanza where "desolation" reads "disolation," and where the motto—"in God is our trust" is spelled with a small "g."

Another strengthening link in the argument which makes Carr godfather of the song and the originator of the title is to be found in his "New Edition" of "The Star Spangled Banner" published in 1821. (See: No. 4.) A notation on the second page of this issue states that it was "Arranged for the P.F. by T.C. the original Publisher." Had the Carrs not been the original publishers, it is not likely that this notation would have been printed by T. Carr seven years later.

No separate title-page.

A Celebrated Patriotic Song, | THE | STAR SPANGLED BANNER | Written (during the Bombardment of Fort McHenry, on the 12th & 13th Septr 1814) by | B.Key Esqr. | Baltimore. Printed and Sold at CARRS Music Store 36 Baltimore Street. | Air. Anacreon in Heaven.

———

No date.

This edition, except for a new and amended title, is printed from the same plates as No. 1 and tallies with that publication in every respect. The dates in the title, however, are incorrect and should read: "the 13th & 14th Septr 1814," and the name of the author is given as "B.Key" instead of "F.S.Key."

No definite record of the date of this edition has come to light. It stands to reason that when the glaring misprint "Pariotic" was discovered in the first issue, it was withdrawn and this new printing with the new and amended title was at once undertaken.

If such was actually the case, then the approximate time of its publication may be derived from an advertisement which appeared in the *Washington Intelligencer* of January 6, 1815, and is reprinted by Sonneck, (page 83):

"STAR SPANGLED BANNER and YE SEAMEN OF COLUMBIA.— Two favorite patriotic songs, this day received and for sale by Richard & Mallory, Bridge Street, Georgetown."

Sonneck, who at the time had never seen copies of these publications, rightly infers that they were music sheet issues. Fortunately the Library of Congress since 1930 has had a copy of:

Ye seamen of Columbia; | a new | naval song. | Written by Wm. Maxwell, Esq. Music by Mr. James Tomlins. | Copy right secured. | Baltimore: published by Neal, Wills and Cole, 174, Market-street.

Between the words "naval" and "song" there is a wood cut of a naval vessel flying a banner on which is printed "Don't give up the ship." The music is printed from type, the printers' names being given at the foot of page [2]—"G. Dobbin and Murphy."

The first verse runs as follows:

> Ye seamen of Columbia;
> Now claim your native sea,
> Break off Britannia's galling chain,
> And set the billows free,

THE STAR SPANGLED BANNER
Published by J. Carr, Baltimore.
Amended Edition. Page [1]. (Bib. No. 1a.)

THE STAR SPANGLED BANNER
Published by J. Carr, Baltimore.
Amended Edition. Page [2]. *(Bib. No. 1a.)*

The spirit of your country calls,
And points where Ocean rolls.

Chorus.
Ye shall reign o'er the main
While its angry surges roar,
Till the sun sets ne'er to rise again,
And the moon looks out no more.

It was evidently issued late in 1814, the Baltimore firm of Neal, Wills and Cole having conducted business from No. 174 Market Street during 1814 and 1815.

This song by the way has little if any connection, musical or literary, with the song "Ye Seamen of Columbia" printed in Rear Admiral Luce's *Naval Songs; A Collection of Original, Selected & Traditional Sea Songs of Sailors and the Sea,* published in 1905 by Wm. A. Pond & Co., New York.

[1814–1816]   No. 2

No separate title-page.

Star Spangled Banner. | PHILADELPHIA | Published by

A. Bacon & Co.   S.4th.Str.
_____

No date.

This Carr-type edition is probably the earliest publication of "The Star Spangled Banner" copied from Carr's original edition.

The title is ornamented with an engraving of the American flag. The publishers' imprint is imperfect; the number "11" in the "11 S. 4th. Str." address is missing in the imprint line.

Music and text, filling two unpaged inside pages, are identical with the Carr No. 1 issue, except that line 6 of the first stanza in the text reads "that our flag still was there" instead of "that our flag was still there." This misplacement of the word "was" has been adopted in many subsequent Carr-type publications. The publishers presumably did not have Carr's original edition to go by and copied either Bacon's issue or one of his followers.

A slight mistake occurs in the music. The last note in the second bar in the bass line of the introduction should read "F" instead of "G."

Neither the name of the author or of the arranger is given.

No. 2a

This edition also appeared with the notation "Price, 25 cts." in the title, and with the plate number "17" in lower margins of pages [1 and 2].

STAR SPANGLED BANNER
Published by A. Bacon & Co., Philadelphia.
Page [1]. (Bib. No. 2.)

flag still was there   O! say does that star spangled banner yet wave,   O'er the

land of the free and the home of the brave   p Sym   pp   p

(2)

On the shore dimly seen thro' the mists of the deep,
Where the foe's haughty host in dread silence reposes,
What is that which the breeze, o'er the towering steep
As it fitfully blows half conceals half discloses;
Now it catches the gleam of the morning's first beam,
In full glory reflected now shines in the stream,
'Tis the star spangled banner O! long may it wave,
O'er the land of the free, and the home of the brave.

(3)

And where is that band who so vauntingly swore.
That the havoc of war and the battle's confusion,
A home and a country shall leave us no more,
Their blood has wash'd out their foul footsteps polluti on
No refuge could save the hireling and slave,
From the terror of flight or the gloom of the grave
And the star spangled banner in triumph doth wave
O'er the land of the free, and the home of the brave.

(4)

O thus be it ever when freemen shall stand,
 Between their lov'd home, and the wars desolation,
Blest with vict'ry and peace, may the heav'n rescued land,
 Praise the Pow'r that hath made and preserv'd us a nation.
Then conquer we must, when our cause it is just,
And this be our motto — In God is our trust;
 And the star spangled banner in triumph shall wave,
 O'er the land of the free and the home of the brave.

FLUTE.

Con
Spirito

STAR SPANGLED BANNER
Published by A. Bacon & Co., Philadelphia.
Page [2]. (*Bib. No. 2.*)

According to Philadelphia city directories of 1814 to 1816 Allyn Bacon was located at No. 11 South Fourth Street under the firm name of Allyn Bacon & Co. or A. Bacon & Co. It was during this period that this edition came into circulation with the A. Bacon & Co. imprint. From 1817 to 1820 the firm is listed as Allyn Bacon or A. Bacon. During the latter part of 1820 Abraham L. Hart joined the firm as partner and from then on the concern is recorded under the name of Bacon & Hart. Their publications carry the same imprint. In 1824 they removed to No. 30 South Fourth Street; Hart withdrew in 1832, and in the following year the firm name Bacon, Weygandt & Co. appears in city records. In 1833 the firm ceased to exist.

It is just possible that the advertisement quoted from the *Washington Intelligencer* in No. 1a refers to this edition. The writer believes, however, that the songs offered for sale by Richard & Mallory were published earlier than the Bacon issue.

[1816–1817]   No. 3

No separate title-page.

THE | STAR SPANGLED BANNER | NEW YORK:
Published by
Geib & Co No 23 Maiden Lane.

———————

No date.

This Carr-type publication, of which music and text fill the two inside pages [2] and 3, is identical with the original Carr edition except that the same misprint occurs in the music as in No. 2 where "G" instead of "F" is used in the bass.

The text is the same as in Carr's edition.
This New York publication was released between 1816 and 1817.

No. 3a

An issue of this edition also appeared with the notation, "25 cents," following the address in the publishers' imprint.

The firm of Geib, makers and dealers in musical instruments and music publishers was founded by John Geib senior. German by birth, he settled for a while in England where he virtually established piano making in the last quarter of the eighteenth century. In 1797 he emigrated to New York with his wife and seven children. New York city directories for 1798 and 1799 record him as "John Geib, organbuilder, First [Street]." For the next two years he appears as John Geib & Co., organ builder, Bowery, corner North Street, and from 1803 to 1814 under the firm name of John Geib & Son at various addresses. He built the first organ for Grace Church, New York. John and Adam, two of his sons also engaged in the making of pianos from 1804 to 1808. Old John Geib died in 1819 in his seventy-fifth year of age, John junior

JOHN GEIB, SENIOR
From the Painting by J. W. Jarvis. From the Estate of Mrs. Mary A. Jaquith, East Orange, N. J.
(By Permission of the Frick Art Reference Library, N. Y.)

JOHN GEIB, JUNIOR
From the Painting by J. W. Jarvis. From the Estate of Mrs. Mary A. Jaquith, East Orange, N. J.
(By Permission of the Frick Art Reference Library, N. Y.)

two years later. Both are buried in St. Paul's churchyard at Vesey Street and Broadway. After 1821 the business was carried on by Adam, and the younger brother William.

In 1816, when the concern moved to No. 23 Maiden Lane, the firm name was changed to John and Adam Geib & Co., or just Geib & Co. Their publications for 1816 and 1817 invariably are imprinted with either one or the other of the above names. William became an active partner in 1818 and the firm assumed the name of J. A. & W. Geib which lasted until 1821, the year John junior died. The brothers continued the business as A. & W. Geib and A. & W. Geib & Co. from 1822 to 1827, when they separated. The New York *Evening Post* for January 2, 1828 carries a notice of dissolution of this partnership. The manufacturing was done by William on Third Avenue and Eleventh Street, and the music business was continued by Adam at No. 23 Maiden Lane. In 1829, Adam took his son-in-law Daniel Walker, later a founder of the Philharmonic Society, into business with him, changing the firm name to Geib & Walker. This partnership was dissolved in 1843, when S. T. Gordon acquired a portion of their catalogue. From then on the firm relinquished music publishing and devoted its energy to making and dealing in piano fortes and other musical instruments.

Adam conducted business for the next four years from No. 73 and No. 71 Third Avenue respectively, but in 1848 he disappears from city records. His second son, William H. Geib, remained at the old Maiden Lane address from 1844 to 1847, and in the following year removed to No. 361 Broadway, where John Jackson Jr. joined him in 1849. The firm name of Geib & Jackson is listed at different Broadway addresses as late as 1858. In 1859 William H. Geib is again recorded as the sole owner of the firm, which existed until 1872.

George Geib, a pianist, writer and teacher in New York, and, according to Brown's *Dictionary of Musicians,* the author of a "Patent Analytical and Grammatical system of teaching the science of the composition of music in all its branches, and the practice of the Pianoforte," printed in New York in 1819, may have been a member of the family. He is listed in New York city directories from 1818 to 1843 as "music store and teacher" at various city addresses. Old John Geib actually had a son George, but according to family tradition he lived in Kentucky and looked after some property his father had bought there. On the other hand, George Senior's son, George H. Geib, is recorded in competition with his cousins as music teacher and dealer in pianos from 1843 to 1872 at different New York city addresses. Neither he nor the other George Geib ever engaged in the music publishing business.

[1821]   No. 4

No separate title-page.

New Edition | STAR SPANGLED BANNER | Written by B. Key, Esqr. | Written during the Bombardment of Fort McHenry— | on the 12 & 13th. Sept. 1814 | Published and Sold by T. CARR, Music Store Baltimore.

————————

STAR SPANGLED BANNER
Published by Thomas Carr, Baltimore.
Page [1]. (Bib. No. 4.)

2

On the shore dimly seen thro' the mists of the deep,
Where the Foe's haughty host in dread silence repo's
What is that which the breeze, o'er the towering steep,
As it fitfully blows, half conceals, half discloses;
Now it catches the gleam of the morning's first beam,
In full glory reflected new shines in the stream,
'Tis the Star spangled Banner, O! long may it wave,
O'er the Land &c.

3

And where is that band who so vauntingly swore
That the havoc of war and the battle's confusion,
A home and a country, shall leave us no more
Their blood has wash'd out their foul footsteps pollution;
No refuge could save the hireling and slave,
From the terror of flight or the gloom of the grave,
And the Star spangled Banner, in trumph doth wave,
O'er the Land &c.

4

O! thus be it ever when freemen shall stand,
Between their lov'd home, and the war's desolation;
Blest with vict'ry and peace, may the Heav'n rescued land,
Praise the Pow'r that hath made and preserv'd us a nation!
Then conquer we must, when our cause it is just,
And this be our motto — In God is our trust;
And the Star spangled Banner, in triumph shall wave,
O'er the Land &c.

For the Flute.

Arranged for the P.F. by T.C. the original Publisher.

STAR SPANGLED BANNER
Published by Thomas Carr, Baltimore.
Page [2]. *(Bib. No. 4.)*

No. date.

Thomas Carr advertised this publication in the Baltimore Federal Gazette under date of February 26, 1821: "A new edition of The Star Spangled Banner with a handsome vignette of the Bombardment of Fort McHenry just published."

Music and text printed from new plates fill two unpaged inside pages. The engraving of the bombardment is underneath the title, above which and on each side is a large star. The tune indication "To Anacreon in Heaven" is omitted, but the faulty date and the wrong initial "B" in Key's name persist.

The music is practically the same as in No. 1, except that a number of small notes have been added in the voice part and in the coda, a few notes have been left out.

The text is the same as in No. 1.

On the lower margin of the second page appears the notation "Arranged for the P. F. by T. C. the original Publisher."

It is interesting to note in this edition Thomas Carr's claim to being the original publisher of the song. The first edition, already gives him credit for the original arrangement of the music.

[1823–1824]   No. 5

No separate title-page.

STAR SPANGLED BANNER. | PHILADELPHIA | Published by J. G. KLEMM. No. 3 S. 3d. St.—Price, 25 cts.

———————

No date.   Plate number 17.

This Carr-type edition is a reissue of the A. Bacon & Co. No. 2a. It is printed from the same plates with the old plate number retained but with the imprint changed to read "J. G. Klemm."

A short resume of the Klemm family history is necessary to show how the publication date of this edition has been fixed between 1823 and 1824.

Johann Gottlob Klemm, the head of a firm of German manufacturers and vendors of musical instruments, came to this country in 1736 and settled in Philadelphia. He was a famous organ builder and worked for a time in New York, where he is known to have built the first American organ for Trinity Church. Two of his sons, John G. and A. F. Klemm, established themselves in Philadelphia in 1818, as music publishers and importers and dealers in musical merchandise. They were located at No. 1 North Fourth Street under the firm name of Klemm & Brother. The business was dissolved in 1822.

John G. Klemm re-established himself in business in the following year. Philadelphia city directories for 1823 and 1824 fail to list him, but Scharf and Westcott in the *History of Philadelphia* state that "this firm [Klemm & Brother] was dissolved in 1823 and John G. Klemm bought out at that time the stock of music and

[70]

plates of Bacon & Hart and removed his store to No. 3 South Third Street, where it remained until about 1825, when he removed to No. 287½ Market Street."

This statement is only partly correct. J. G. Klemm did not buy out the complete Bacon & Hart music stock and plates, but he did acquire the old stock and some old plates which Bacon had published early in his career. During the period of 1823 and 1824 he reprinted all of Bacon's early issues, one of which was the "Star Spangled Banner." It is interesting to compare the Bacon publications with the reprints. All of them, like No. 11, the "Washington March," and No. 12 "President March," carry Bacon's plate number with the substitution of the Klemm imprint.

From 1825 to 1831, the city records place Klemm at No. 287½ Market Street (High Street). After this the brothers got together again under the old title Klemm & Brother, and for the next eight years conducted their "pianoforte warehouse" at the old address. They moved twice: first to No. 275 Market Street where they remained until 1856 and in the following year to No. 705 Market Street, where the firm was still to be found in 1866.

[1823–1826]   No. 6

No separate title-page.

STAR SPANGLED BANNER | Baltimore. Published and Sold by GEO: WILLIG.

No date.

This Carr-type edition is a single-page sheet-song publication, an adaptation of the Bacon (No. 2) edition. The text carries the Bacon variant, the misplaced "was" in line 6 in the first stanza.

The music is shortened; several bars in the coda are omitted and the entire flute arrangement left out. No arranger's name is given.

Unfortunately one can do no more than conjecture the date of this imprint. Diligent search and examination of the publisher's early output seem to establish the fact that George Willig's publications of that period were for the most part single-page issues. The "Star Spangled Banner," no doubt, was one of them. The majority of his early publications were undated and without a street address. Now and then one of his pieces appeared with copyright date, or street number. One of these, "The Castilian Maid" has the copyright notice "Melody Sketches No. 1. Copyright secured the fourth day of August 1823." Another, "And since you leave me," was copyrighted December 6, 1824. This vocal number also bears his street address, No. 71 Market Street. These are, however, the exceptions and not the rule.

George Willig was the son of the pioneer music dealer and publisher of the same name who had settled in Philadelphia in 1794. The younger Willig was born in Philadelphia in 1794. At the close of 1822 he came to Baltimore and started a music store at No. 95 Market Street (Baltimore Street). He bought part of the stock and

STAR SPANGLED BANNER

BALTIMORE, Published and Sold by GEO: WILLIG.

(2)

On the shore dimly seen thro' the mists of the deep,
  Where the foe's haughty host in dread silence reposes
What is that which the breeze, o'er the towering steep
  As it fitfully blows half conceals half discloses,
Now it catches the gleam of the morning's first beam,
In full glory reflected now shines in the stream,
  'Tis the star spangled banner O! long may it wave,
  O'er the land of the free, and the home of the brave.

(3)

And where is that band who so vauntingly swore,
  That the havoc of war and the battle's confusion,
A home and a country shall leave us no more,
  Their blood has wash'd out their foul footsteps pollution,
No refuge could save the hireling and slave,
From the terror of flight or the gloom of the grave,
  And the star spangled banner in triumph doth wave
  O'er the land of the free, and the home of the brave.

(4)

O thus be it ever, when freemen shall stand,
  Between their lov'd home, and the wars desolation,
Blest with vict'ry and peace, may the heav'n rescued land,
  Praise the Power that hath made and preserv'd us a nation
Then conquer we must, when our cause it is just,
And this be our motto "In God is our trust",
  And the star spangled banner in triumph shall wave,
  O'er the land of the free and the home of the brave.

STAR SPANGLED BANNER
Published by George Willig, Baltimore.
(Bib. No. 6.)

plates of Thomas Carr and commenced to publish vocal and instrumental pieces of the single-page type. He did not use a uniform imprint, but varied it from "G" to "Geo." to "George" Willig.

His business is not listed in any of the city directories until 1824, but an advertisement in the *Federal Gazette* of October 2, 1823 announces that Willig has: "removed his store to 71 Baltimore St. opposite Holliday." In 1826 he is recorded at No. 74 Baltimore Street.

At that time a change is noted in his imprint line to "G.," "Geo.," or George Willig "Jr.," which was added, in all probability, to distinguish his publications from those of his father who still was in business in Philadelphia. In 1829 he used the new imprint line more frequently and also added the "Jr." to his copyright notice. He did not, however, stick closely to the new policy. A number of his later publications, from 1826 to 1831, appeared without the "Jr.," "Jun." or "Junior," tagged on to his imprint.

This data is of great assistance in determining the date of the publication. When the "Star Spangled Banner" song-sheet is compared with Willig's early publications, which bear copyright dates, the conclusion that they are of one type and one period is irresistible. It is also borne out by the fact that he issued the same music-sheet sometime later with the amended publisher's imprint line "Geo. Willig Jr."

[1826–1831]   No. 6a

No separate title-page.

STAR SPANGLED BANNER | Baltimore. Published by GEO: WILLIG Jr.

————————

No date.

This Carr-type single-page edition is a reissue of No. 6, printed from the same plates. The only mark distinguishing it from the original issue is the "Jr." which has been added to the publisher's name on his imprint line.

The lack of uniformity in Willig's early publications, which has been fully discussed in No. 6, makes it impossible definitely to determine the date of this piece. Since the "Jr." came into use in 1826 and served intermittently until 1831, it is safe to set the time of this reissue between 1826 and 1831.

6b

A variant of No. 6a, a copy of which is in the Library of Congress, appeared with plate number "1578." It was evidently issued in December, 1843, according to corresponding plate numbers on copyrighted Willig publications. The publisher used plate number "1444" in November, 1843, and in February, 1844, number "1850."

[73]

GEORGE WILLIG, JUNIOR
From a Painting in the Possession of Miss Eugenia C. Willig, Baltimore.

No separate title-page.

THE STAR SPANGLED BANNER. | Published by John Cole, Baltimore.

No date.   Plate number 152.

This Carr-type edition, of which music and text fill two inside pages—pp. [1] and 2—is copied from the Carr "New Edition" (No. 4) and is practically the same except that the music is redivided from the original 6/4 into 3/4 time.

The flute arrangement is omitted.

The title is ornamented with an engraving of an artillery firing scene showing the flag, with twelve stars, floating over the smoke. A number of ships are seen in the background.

The plate number is found on the lower margins of both pages.

In the text the misplaced word "was" appears in line 6 of first stanza; in line 3 of the same verse the word "broad" was omitted. That line reads: "Whose stripes and bright stars etc. ." instead of "Whose broad stripes and bright stars etc. ." This variant has been copied in subsequent publications.

There is no doubt that this edition was issued in 1825. Fortunately the publisher supplied his imprints with corresponding plate numbers, and comparison of these, with his copyrighted publications, invariably furnishes the correct date.

The earliest Cole imprint with an actual copyright date is plate number 30, May 4th, 1822. Another, somewhat later in the same year, is number 63. In 1825 we find several copyrighted pieces issued with their respective plate numbers: the song "Come down to the Latice; A Serenade composed . . . by C. Meineke" bears the plate number 154 and the notice: "Entered according to Act of Congress August 13, 1825 by John Cole of the State of Maryland."

Since the plate numbers 152 ("The Star Spangled Banner") and "154" are so close together, there can be no question that the two pieces were published almost simultaneously.

John Cole was twelve years old when in 1786 he came to Baltimore with his family from England. He was destined to become one of the leading music publishers of that city. By all accounts Cole was a most interesting personality. A printer by trade, a proficient clarinet player and an all around musician, he was noted for his compilation of tune-books for church use, to which he contributed such hymn tunes of his own as "Geneva," ("When all thy mercies, o my God . . etc."). He was present at the battle of Bladensburg (1814) as the leader of the military band, the "Independent Blues." He and his brother Samuel were choir leaders in St. Paul's and Christ Churches, where John met and formed a friendship with the Carrs, who were organists in those churches.

In 1804 Cole set up in the book trade. His name appears in Baltimore city directories under: "Cole & Hewes, booksellers, 14 S. Calvert St." They, no doubt, conformed with the custom of the day and carried music and related merchandise as

JOHN COLE
From a Daguerreo-type, Property of Miss Helen M. Simonton, Baltimore.

THE STAR SPANGLED BANNER
Published by John Cole, Baltimore.
Page [1]. *(Bib. No. 7.)*

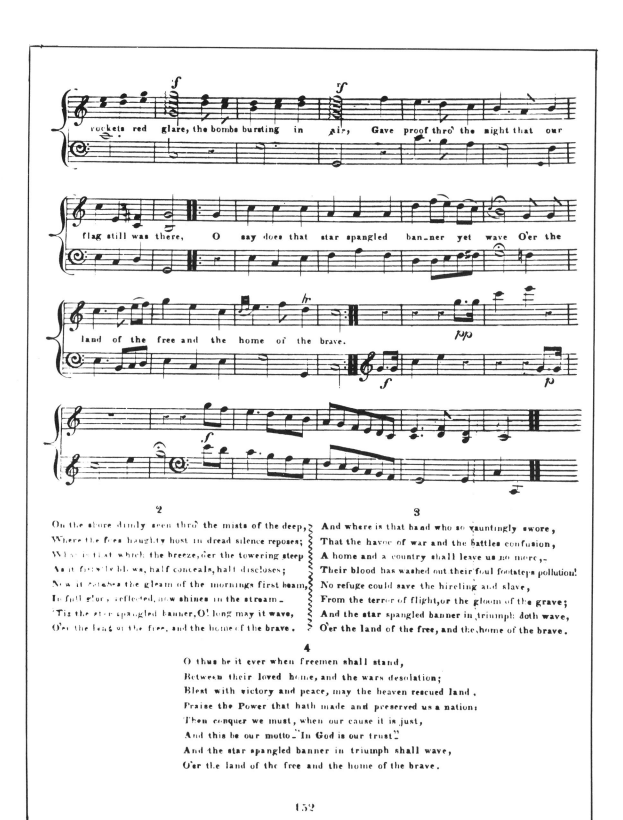

rockets red glare, the bombs bursting in air, Gave proof thro' the night that our

flag still was there, O say does that star spangled ban—ner yet wave O'er the

land of the free and the home of the brave.

2

On the shore dimly seen thro' the mists of the deep,
Where the foes haughty host in dread silence reposes;
What is that which the breeze, o'er the towering steep
As it fitfully blows, half conceals, half discloses;
Now it catches the gleam of the mornings first beam,
In full glory, reflected, now shines in the stream—
'Tis the star spangled banner, O! long may it wave,
O'er the land of the free, and the home of the brave.

3

And where is that band who so vauntingly swore,
That the havoc of war and the battles confusion,
A home and a country shall leave us no more,—
Their blood has washed out their foul footsteps pollution!
No refuge could save the hireling and slave,
From the terror of flight, or the gloom of the grave;
And the star spangled banner in triumph doth wave,
O'er the land of the free, and the home of the brave.

4

O thus be it ever when freemen shall stand,
Between their loved home, and the wars desolation;
Blest with victory and peace, may the heaven rescued land,
Praise the Power that hath made and preserved us a nation:
Then conquer we must, when our cause it is just,
And this be our motto—"In God is our trust."
And the star spangled banner in triumph shall wave,
O'er the land of the free and the home of the brave.

152

THE STAR SPANGLED BANNER
Published by John Cole, Baltimore.
Page [2]. *(Bib. No. 7.)*

TITLE-PAGE OF "BUY A BROOM"
Published by John Cole, Baltimore ca. 1835. Showing John Cole's music store.
(Courtesy of Mr. A. B. Hunt, Brooklyn, N. Y.)

well as books. How long the firm remained in business cannot be ascertained. City directories fail to mention them further; however, in 1814 and 1815 the firm of Neal, Wills and Cole, booksellers, is listed at No. 174 Baltimore Street, and in 1816 re-appears at No. 14 South Calvert Street, where John Cole, bookseller, is also recorded as living and conducting business from 1814 to 1815. John Cole did not start music publishing of his own until 1822, when he opened a music store at No. 125½ Baltimore (Market) Street, having acquired some of the stock of music and plates belonging to Thomas Carr, who sold out at that time and left Baltimore for Philadelphia. In 1827 Cole removed to No. 137 Baltimore Street where he remained until May 8, 1839, when Frederick D. Benteen bought him out and continued in business at the same address. In 1835 John Cole associated himself for a while with his son, who also was a good musician. A number of publications appear with the imprint "John Cole & Son" and also "George F. Cole." The son, whose full name was George Frederick Handel Cole, kept a music store at No. 10 N. Holliday Street in 1840. John Cole, after relinquishing his business in Baltimore Street, is recorded in 1840 at No. 1 North Charles Street as a dealer in pianos. Thereafter his address (no occupation given) is listed at Lombard Street. He died on August 17, 1855 at the ripe old age of eighty-one.

(A Cole publication in the writer's collection, "Buy a Broom," an engraved and hand colored song in sheet-form issued in 1835 or thereabouts, shows his store-front at No. 137 Market Street. The picture, which was engraved by Medairy & Bannerman, is said to represent Madame Vestris, the famous English singer and actress, standing in front of Cole's store offering brooms for sale. The idea of this cut apparently was taken from an earlier English lithographed music title made by M. Gauci, which reads: "Buy a Broom, the poetry by J. R. Planche, the music by Henry R. Bishop." The illustration shows Miss Love offering her brooms in front of No. 20 Soho Square, London, the establishment of the music publishers Goulding & D'Almaine. Mention of this title-page is made because it has been used by other publishers of the song with the substitution of the particular publisher's shop window for Cole's. (See song published by E. S. Mesier, Wall Street, New York about 1830).

[1832–1839]   No. 8

No separate title-page.

THE | STAR SPANGLED BANNER, | A Popular | NATIONAL AIR, |
    Arranged with an Accompaniment for the | Piano Forte. |
New York, Firth & Hall, 1 Franklin Square.

———————

No date.

This edition is the earliest publication of the song not copied from the Carr editions or from any of the Carr-type issues.
    Music and text fill pages [1]–3.
    The music is an arrangement in 6/4 time in the key of C major. Carr's melody
[80]

THE STAR SPANGLED BANNER
Published by Firth & Hall, New York.
Page [1]. *(Bib. No. 8.)*

THE STAR SPANGLED BANNER
Published by Firth & Hall, New York.
Page [2]. *(Bib. No. 8.)*

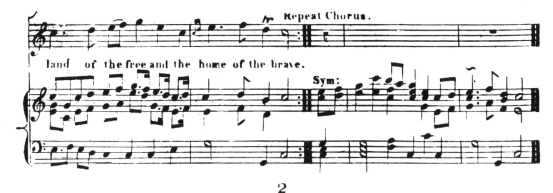

land   of the free and the home of the brave.

2

On the shore dimly seen thro' the mists of the deep,

Where the foe's haughty host in dead silence reposes

What is, that which the breeze, o'er the towering steep

As it fitfully blows half conceals half discloses;

Now it catches the gleam, of the morning's first beam,

In full glory reflected now shines in the stream,

And the star spangled banner O! long may it wave,

O'er the land of the free, and the home of the brave.

3

And where is that band who so vauntingly swore,

That the havoc of war and the battle's confusion,

A home and a country shall leave us no more,

Their blood has wash'd out their foul footsteps pollution

No refuge could save, the hireling and slave,

From the terror of flight or the gloom of the grave

And the star spangl'd banner in triumph doth wave

O'er the land of the free, and the home of the brave.

4

O thus be it ever when freemen shall stand,

Between their lov'd home, and the wars desolation,

Blest with vict'ry and peace, may the heav'n rescued land,

Praise the pow'r that hath made and preserv'd us a nation.

Then conquer we must, when our cause it is just,

And this be our motto— In God is our trust;

And the star spangled banner in triumph shall wave,

O'er the land of the free and the home of the brave.

Star Spangle. 3.

THE STAR SPANGLED BANNER
Published by Firth & Hall, New York.
Page [3]. *(Bib. No. 8.)*

version is retained, but a modern right hand piano accompaniment has been added and a more elaborate bass part substituted. The arranger's name is not given. The flute arrangement is missing.

The text carries the misplaced word "was" in line 6 of first stanza. Verso of page 3 is blank.

No. 8a

Some copies of this edition bear the notation "Star Spangle.3." on the lower margins of pages 2 and 3. Verso of page 3 is blank.

Sonneck, in *The Star Spangled Banner* (1914), describes a copy of this publication which is in the Library of Congress, and places the approximate time of its appearance between the years 1832 and 1839. He bases his conclusion on the fact that the firm of Firth and Hall was not at No. 1 Franklin Square before 1832, and that the copy under examination bears the stamp of "W. E. Millet's Music Saloon, 375 Broadway, N. Y." Sonneck says: "According to city directories, Millet was at this address from 1836–37 to 1838–39. From 1839–40 on, his address was at 329 Broadway. Obviously then, the piece must have been published before 1840." The date may be more definitely fixed only if copies carrying some other tell-tale marks come to light. (My own copy, although signed and dated "Edw. L. Davenport, Chestnut Street Theatre 1839" does not help in this case).

The New York firm of Firth and Hall, music publishers and dealers, was founded in 1821 by John Firth and William Hall. They established themselves at No. 362 Pearl Street and for the next ten years remained in that neighborhood occupying different houses in close proximity. From 1823 to 1826 they are listed in city directories at No. 358 Pearl Street and from 1827–1828 to 1829–1831 at Nos. 358 and 360 Pearl Street. In 1832 their place of business was removed to No. 1 Franklin Square. After a time Sylvanus B. Pond joined the firm as partner, and the firm name was changed to Firth, Hall & Pond In 1847 when Hall withdrew and formed the firm of William Hall & Son at No. 239 Broadway, the old concern dissolved.

Firth & Pond reorganized again in 1848, and with S. B. Pond's son, William A. Pond, as partner, formed a new company under the name of Firth, Pond & Co.

It is difficult to follow the firm of Firth & Hall from 1832 through to the time of its dissolution since the city records and copyright entries do not agree.

New York directories list the firm as Firth, Hall & Pond in 1833, and again from 1843 to 1845; but all copyright entries from 1833 to September 15, 1845 are registered as Firth & Hall or Firth, Hall & Co. Information from the Library of Congress confirms Sonneck's statement about the change from Firth & Hall to Firth, Hall & Pond between September 15 and September 24, 1845. There is, however, one isolated entry under Firth, Hall & Pond on December 31, 1833.

These irregularities lead one to suspect that S. B. Pond, whose entrance into the firm was recorded as having taken place in 1845, may well have been a partner long before that time. Daniel Spilane, in his *History of the American Pianoforte*, N. Y. 1890, claims that: "towards 1840 Firth & Hall became Firth, Hall & Pond,

[84]

JOHN FIRTH
The Firth, Pond & Co. Building, No. 1 Franklin Square, New York.

owing to the accession of Sylvanus B. Pond, of Albany, who since 1827 had been connected with the Meachams in the retail piano trade."

It is also noteworthy that in 1844–1845 Firth & Hall, and in 1846–1847 Firth, Hall & Pond are listed at No. 239 Broadway, and that William Hall & Son appear in the publishing business at this address.

Perhaps this is enough to show that it is unsafe to base any argument on the form of a firm name alone and that street addresses are often misleading.

[1834–1836]   No. 9

No separate title-page.

THE STAR SPANGLED BANNER | BOSTON: Published by C. BRADLEE 107 Washington Street.

———————

No date.

This Carr-type edition is an exact copy of the Cole publication. Music and text fill two inside pages—page [1] and 2. It has all the characteristics of No. 7, except that the engraving of the artillery scene is not printed in this issue.

The date of this Boston publication has been derived from information obtained by Mr. William Arms Fisher, Vice President of the Oliver Ditson Company, Inc., and data found in Boston city records and on copyrighted pieces of this publisher.

"Charles Bradlee," according to Mr. William Arms Fisher, "began music publishing in 1829 at No. 164 Washington Street, Boston, and continued at various addresses until 1846, after which his name disappears from Boston city directories. His catalog was taken over by Oliver Ditson."

Bradlee seems to have been constantly on the move. On November 1, 1833 the Boston Transcript records a disaster at the building at No. 164 Washington Street: "About half past 3 o'clock this morning fire was discovered in the cellar of the building. . . . Mr. Charles Bradlee lost a large portion of his sheet music and plates." His name is not listed in 1834 but appears in 1835 and 1836 at No. 2 Sweetser Court. This must have been his residence, for several imprints, copyrighted in 1834 and 1836 and bearing the No. 107 Washington Street address, indicate that he conducted his business during this time at the above location. From 1837 to 1844 inclusive, he lived at No. 12 School Street. His copyrighted publications during this period appear in 1837 with the No. 135 Washington Street business address. How long he remained there, however, cannot positively be stated, but his last shop, according to the imprint on his dated pieces, was located at No. 184 Washington Street, where he appears in 1845 and 1846 as C. Bradlee & Co.

No. 107 Washington Street is a famous address in American Music Publishing. It was here that Oliver Ditson first became an independent publisher in 1835. Between 1835 and 1836, Ditson and Bradlee were neighbors and may even have collaborated, although we have no proof of this.

[86]

No separate title-page.

STAR SPANGLED BANNER | NEW YORK, ATWILL Publisher, 201 Broadway.

No date.

This single-sheet publication is copied from the George Willig edition (No. 6) and tallies with it in every detail except for the following inaccuracies in the text: in the second stanza the word "silence" in line 2 reads "silance," and in the next line the word "which" is spelled "wich"; in the fourth verse the word "God" in "God is our trust" is spelled with a small "g."

The date of this issue may be placed between the years 1834 and 1843, the period during which Joseph F. Atwill (see: No. 15, of this bibliography) conducted his music store at No. 201 Broadway, N. Y. C. Although the theory that this undated edition appeared in the thirties and before 1840 cannot be proved, it is safe to assume that the publisher issued this piece before 1843 at which time he published his *Collection of National Songs of America,* arranged for the piano by Francis H. Brown, and containing a new musical setting of "The Star Spangled Banner" (see: No. 15). This collection of favorite patriotic airs enjoyed considerable popularity at the time, particularly "The Star Spangled Banner" version, which in the course of time was repeatedly reprinted by different publishers, and Atwill would scarcely have encumbered it with any old versions.

No separate title-page.

THE | STAR SPANGLED BANNER. | NEW YORK Published by Hewitt & Jaques 239 Broadway.

No date.

The music and text of this Carr-type edition fills two unpaged inside pages and is identical with the Geib edition (No. 3) from which, apparently, it was copied.

This edition, like all of the early "Star-Spangled Banner" issues, bears no copyright notice. The date of its appearance, therefore, falls into the period when Hewitt & Jaques were associated in business.

According to the pamphlet *Music Publishers in New York City before 1850,* issued by the New York Public Library in 1917, Hewitt & Edward I. Jaques are listed in the city directories between 1839 and 1841 at No. 239 Broadway. That the firm actually went under that name as early as 1837 is apparent from pieces they published and copyrighted in that year. One such publication is "Williams Light Infantry Quick Step," composed by Sam A. Cooper. This has the Hewitt & Jaques imprint at No. 239 Broadway and the copyright line: "Entered according to act of Congress in the year 1837 by Hewitt & Jaques in the Clerks Office of the District Court of the Southern District of New York." Another is Henry Russell's "A Life on the Ocean Wave" with the Hewitt & Jaques imprint and copyright notice and date 1838.

James Long Hewitt, second son of James Hewitt, the early American musician and publisher, was brought up in the music business in New York. At an early age he was sent for by James A. Dickson, manager of the Boston Theatre on Federal Street who opened a music store at No. 36 Market Street. Hewitt was made a partner, and four years later Dickson gave him the entire business. Boston directories list him from 1825 to 1829 under the firm name of J. L. Hewitt & Co., at the above address.

In the New York Public Library pamphlet already referred to, James L. Hewitt & Co. is recorded in 1830–31 at No. 137 Broadway. Publications of James L. Hewitt & Co., however, contradict this statement. "I see them on their winding way," composed by B. Hime, was published according to the imprint line, by the Hewitt firm in New York at No. 129 Broadway. This must have been during the time from 1825 to 1829, when Hewitt was active in Boston, because a number of pieces contain both his Boston and New York address. The imprint on "Comin' Thro' The Rye," for instance, is: "Boston, Published by James L. Hewitt & Co. at their Music Saloon No. 36 Market St. and No. 129 Broadway, New York." Another song, "The Lavender Girl," appeared with the 129 Broadway, New York address and the Boston address following.

A very important song of that period, which establishes the fact that Hewitt kept a shop in New York at least as early as 1827 is "The Minstrels returned from the war, as Sung by Mr. C. W. Taylor—Written and Composed by J. H. H." The imprint gives the Boston (36 Market Street) and the New York (129 Broadway) addresses. This is the first song written and composed by John Hill Hewitt, a brother of the publisher. The original manuscript in the Library of Congress has the following penciled memorandum by the composer.

"This song, as crude as it is, was one of my first musical efforts. It was composed in 1825 in the village of Greenville, S. C. now a city of 10,000 souls. When I returned to the North, I took this book with me to Boston. My brother James was a music publisher. I gave him a copy to publish—he did it very reluctantly—did not think it worthy of a copyright. It was eagerly taken up by the public, and established my reputation as a ballad composer. It was sung all over the world—and my brother, not securing the right, told me that he missed making at least $10,000."

According to John Tasker Howard, in his book *Our American Music*, Hewitt "returned to the North because of his father's death in 1827." It may be in that year that J. L. Hewitt established his New York branch of the business.

From 1830 to 1835 he was at No. 137 Broadway as James L. Hewitt & Co. His "Music Store" is included in an old engraving showing "The City Hotel, New York," in 1830. From 1836 to 1843 he conducted business from No. 239 Broadway. It was

[88]

during this period that Edward I. Jaques became a partner, and the firm name was changed to Hewitt & Jaques, as has already been noted. Jaques seems to have relinquished his partnership in 1841, and until 1843 the firm again used the name James L. Hewitt & Co. For the next three years, until 1847 when Hewitt retired from business, the firm at various Broadway addresses went under the name of James L. Hewitt. Hewitt died in 1853 at the age of forty-six.

[1838]   No. 12

No separate title-page.

Collective title: YANKEE DOODLE | & | STAR SPANGLED BANNER | Philada. OSBOURN'S MUSIC SALOON, 30 S. 4th. St.

No date.   Plate number 128.

This Carr-type edition is an issue of a collection of three songs. The "STAR SPANGLED BANNER" appears on page [4].

YANKEE DOODLE is printed on the outside page [1], and HAIL COLUMBIA on the two inside pages [2] and [3]. The caption title on page [2] reads: "The popular National Air, | HAIL COLUMBIA | WITH | YANKEE DOODLE & STAR SPANGLED BANNER | Composed & Simplified | FOR THE | PIANO FORTE." The publisher's imprint is the same as on page [1]. All three songs carry the same plate number.

The caption title on page [4] reads: STAR SPANGLED BANNER.

Music and words are the same as the Willig edition (No. 6) and apparently are copied from it.

In line 3 of the second stanza of the text the word "breeze" is misspelt "breze."

According to plate numbers examined on copyrighted music printed by this Philadelphia publisher, the publication appeared in 1838. This date is verified as closely as possible by Osbourn's edition of Charles Jarvis's "The Philadelphia Quadrilles," plate number 132, which was deposited for copyright on September 27, 1838. Preceding and subsequent plate numbers on Osbourn's publications on file in the Library of Congress are as follows: 1836 plate number 20 and 25; 1837 plate number 30; 1839 plate number 145 to 200 etc..

James G. Osbourn and Frederick W. Miller, Philadelphia musicians, music dealers and publishers, started business in 1832 at No. 35 North Fourth Street under the firm name of Miller & Osbourn. In 1834 Osbourn withdrew and Miller carried on alone at the same address until 1850. After that time his name is not listed in Philadelphia city directories.

Osbourn opened his "Music Saloon" in 1836 at No. 30 South Fourth Street, moving in 1843 to No. 27 South Fourth Street, and in 1844 to No. 112 South Third Street, where he remained until 1847. From 1848 on his name is recorded for a number of years as music teacher at No. 428 North Sixth Street.

[89]

No separate title-page.

THE STAR SPANGLED BANNER | Published by Geo. Willig Jr, Baltimore.

No date.   Plate number 152.

This Carr-type publication is a reissue of the Cole edition. It is printed from the Cole plates with the plate number retained, but with the publisher's imprint line changed to read "Geo. Willig Jr." Otherwise it answers the description of No. 7 in every detail.

The knowledge that this edition was published between 1839 to 1841 may be derived from the following facts. Cole retired from business in 1839, at which time he sold his stock to F. D. Benteen and others. Willig apparently acquired the plates for "The Star Spangled Banner," which he reprinted, retaining the Cole plate number and substituting his own imprint.

A copy in the writer's collection with the signature "Catherine Ingersole, October 9th, 1841." serves as evidence that the publication was not issued after 1841.

No separate title-page.

THE CELEBRATED NATIONAL SONG | THE STAR SPANGLED BANNER |
A. FIOT, Philadelphia.

No date.

This Carr-type edition of which music and text fill two unpaged inside pages is identical with the Philadelphia edition of A. Bacon & Co. (No. 2) and apparently was copied from it.

The music has the misprint "G" for "F" in the bass of the second bar of the introduction, and in the text, the misplaced "was" appears in line 6 of the first stanza.

The notation "Star Spangled Banner" appears under the flute arrangement in lower margin of page [2].

The probable publication date of this edition must be surmised from the publisher's imprint and the typography, for Fiot never used plate numbers. Examination of some of his output during the year he began publishing, 1834, shows that his imprint was invariably simply "A. Fiot, Philadelphia." Not until later did he add his street address. The typography, too, is typical of that used in the thirties and forties, when the inside titles of sheet music were ordinary straight letters stamped on a metal plate from a punch. So that, although there is insufficient evidence to fix the date very accurately, we can safely assume that Fiot published the "Star Spangled Banner" before 1853 and possibly in the early forties. The writer's copy bears a pencilled name and the date: "Jan. 1, '54" written in the upper right hand corner of page [1].

August Fiot, who became a Philadelphia publisher of some renown, began business in 1834 at No. 264 High Street under the firm name of A. Fiot. A year later Leopold Meignen, a prolific composer and splendid musician, became his partner at the above address, changing the firm name to Fiot, Meignen & Co. In 1837 they removed to No. 217 Chestnut Street and two years later separated.

Meignen appears at the 217 Chestnut Street address until 1842 under the firm name of Ld. Meignen and Ld. Meignen & Co. In 1843 his name as publisher disappears, but from 1849 to 1855 he is listed as a music teacher at No. 27 Powell Street. Meignen was connected with the Musical Fund Society where, succeeding Charles Hupfeld, he conducted the orchestra for a long period.

Fiot, under the name of A. Fiot, was engaged in the musical instrument trade and in selling and publishing music at No. 169 Chestnut Street from 1840 to 1853, after which date his name disappears from Philadelphia city records. John E. Gould, of No. 164 Chestnut Street bought his music and catalogue.

1843   No. 15

Collective title-page.

ATWILL'S | COLLECTION OF NATIONAL SONGS OF AMERICA | No. 5. | THE STAR SPANGLED BANNER." | The Words written by | FRANCIS S. KEYS, ESQ. | (OF BALTIMORE.) | The Symphonies and Accompaniments | Composed & Arranged | AND RESPECTFULLY INSCRIBED | TO | the Officers of the Army and Navy | OF THE | UNITED STATES, | by | FRANCIS H. BROWN. |

No.
1. LAND OF WASHINGTON!   Price   4. HUZZA! HUZZA!
2. HAIL COLUMBIA!   25 Cts. ea.   5. STAR SPANGLED BANNER!
3. OUR FLAG IS THERE!   Nett.   6. YANKEE DOODLE!

NEW YORK. | Published by ATWILL, 201 Broadway. |
Entered according to Act of Congress AD 1843 by Jos. F. Atwill in the Clerks Office of the District Court of the Southern Dist. of New York.

———————

Copyrighted.

This publication was deposited for copyright on November 29, 1843.

No. 5. ["]THE STAR SPANGLED BANNER"—Key's name appears as Francis S. "Keys" on the title-page, verso of which is blank.

Words and music are printed on pages [3]–[5]. Verso of page [5] is blank.

The caption title on page [3] reads: THE STAR SPANGLED BANNER! | Note by the Publisher—This song was supposed to have been written by a prisoner of war, on board the Brittish [!] fleet, on the morning after the unsuccessful bombardment of Fort McHenry, in the second war with England, declared in the year

ATWILL'S

COLLECTION OF NATIONAL SONGS OF AMERICA.

Nº 5,

THE STAR SPANGLED BANNER.

The Words written by

FRANCIS S. KEYS, ESQ,

(OF BALTIMORE)

The Symphonies and Accompaniments

Composed & Arranged

AND RESPECTFULLY INSCRIBED

— TO —

the Officers of the Army and Navy

OF THE

UNITED STATES,

by

FRANCIS H. BROWN.

Nº 1. LAND OF WASHINGTON!	4. HUZZA! HUZZA!
.. 2. HAIL COLUMBIA!	5. STAR SPANGLED BANNER!
.. 3. OUR FLAG IS THERE!	6. YANKEE DOODLE!

{ *Price* 25 Cts ea *Nett* }

NEW YORK

Published by **ATWILL** 201 Broadway

Entered according to Act of Congress D 1843 by Jos F. Atwill in the Clerks Office of the District Court of the Southern Dist of New York

---

THE STAR SPANGLED BANNER
Published by Atwill, New York.
Title-page. (Bib. No. 15.)

THE STAR SPANGLED BANNER!

Note by the Publisher. This song was supposed to have been written by a prisoner of war, on board the Brittish fleet, on the morning after the unsuccessful bombardment of Fort McHenry, in the second war with England, declared in the year 1812. This copy of the words is authentic, as it was submitted to the Author, and revised and corrected by him a few months previous to his death which occurred in 1843.

THE STAR SPANGLED BANNER
Published by Atwill, New York.
Page [3]. *(Bib. No. 15.)*

THE STAR SPANGLED BANNER
Published by Atwill, New York.
Page [4]. *(Bib. No. 15.)*

ban - ner yet wave O'er the land of the free, and the home of the brave!

2

On the shore dimly seen thro' the mist of the deep,
Where the foe's haughty host in dread silence reposes,
What is that which the breeze, o'er the towering steep,
As it fitfully blows, half conceals, half discloses,
Now it catches the gleam of the morning's first beam,
Its full glory reflected now shines on the stream!
'Tis the star-spangled banner! oh, long may it wave
O'er the land of the free, and home of the brave!

3

And where is the band who so vauntingly swore,
'Mid the havoc of war and the battle's confusion,
A home and a country they'd leave us no more!
Their blood has wash'd out their foul footstep's pollution!
No refuge could save the hireling and slave,
From the terror of flight, or the gloom of the grave,
And the star-spangled banner in triumph doth wave,
O'er the land of the free, and the home of the brave!

4

Oh! thus be it ever when freemen shall stand,
Between their lov'd home and the war's desolation,
Blest with vict'ry and peace, may the heav'n rescued land
Praise the Power that hath made and preserv'd us a nation!
Then conquer we must, for our cause it is just!
And this be our motto, "In God is our trust!"
And the star-spangled banner in triumph shall wave
O'er the land of the free, and the home of the brave!

THE STAR SPANGLED BANNER
Published by Atwill, New York.
Page [5]. *(Bib. No. 15.)*

1812. This copy of the words is authentic, as it was submitted to the Author; and revised and corrected by him a few months previous to his death which occurred in 1843."

The textual variation differs from all existing Key manuscripts, as well as from the early printings of the poem. Line 3 in the third verse reads: "A home and a country they'd leave us no more" for "A home and a country shall (or should) leave us no more." Whether Key actually made that change, as is claimed in the publisher's notice, is difficult to say. It is not likely that it is an error since there were many editions in circulation which carried the broadside version adapted by Carr, and subsequent issues of the song copied this Atwill variation. In line 6 of the first stanza the word "was" is placed correctly.

The music is an original arrangement for voice and piano accompaniment in 6/4 time in the key of B-flat major.

This edition of "The Star Spangled Banner" seems to have been in demand. Within the next twenty years it was reprinted by different publishers who used and resold the original plates.

No. 15a

The Atwill edition was also issued in collective form. All six numbers with their respective title-pages as described above were published together with a special lithographed title cover bearing an eagle, a medallion of Washington, the Capitol, American flags and historical scenes. The cover reads: "ATWILL'S EDITION | OF | THE | NATIONAL SONGS | OF | AMERICA, | ARRANGED | for the | PIANO-FORTE | BY | FRANCIS H. BROWN. | NEW-YORK, | Published at | ATWILL'S MUSIC REPOSITORY, | No. 201 Broadway. | FIRST SERIES. | PRICE $1.50 NETT. | Lith. of Lewis & Brown 37 John St. N. Y." The publisher's copyright notice, repeated on the lower margin, is the same as the one printed on the bottom of each title-page of the six songs.

In this set, however, the music is printed on verso of the original (inside) title-page, which gives this piece two inside and one outside pages. (A copy of this scarce set of national songs from which this collation has been made was found in a collection of music owned by Mrs. Charles Eckerson, of Leonia, N. J.)

Joseph F. Atwill was active in the music publishing business in New York from 1833 to 1849. He commenced business at No. 137 Broadway, and in 1834 moved to No. 201 Broadway, where he remained until 1847. In 1848 he removed to No. 300 Broadway, and a year later was succeeded by Samuel C. Jollie, who carried on the business at the same place. Atwill, meanwhile, emigrated to San Francisco, and became the pioneer music publisher of California. Campbell and Hoogs San Francisco and Sacramento City directory, issued in March, 1850, lists: "Atwill's pianoforte, music and commission store, 158 Washington Street, corner of dupont, near the plaza. Joseph F. Atwill." In 1851–1852 he is recorded at Clay Street—Post Office

BROADWAY SIGHTS.

View on Broadway, near St Pauls Church

As Sung with great Applause by

MR. LATHAM,

at the

Grand Concerts,

AT

NIBLO'S GARDEN.

written and arranged by

W. H. LATHAM.

Price 50 c.ts

NEW YORK,
Published at ATWILL'S, MUSIC SALOON, 201, Broadway

TITLE-PAGE OF "BROADWAY SIGHTS"
Published by Atwill, New York, 1835. Showing Atwill's Establishment, No. 201 Broadway.

FRANCIS H. BROWN. TITLE-PAGE OF "I'LL LOVE THEE IN THE SPRING TIME"
Published by William Hall & Son, New York, 1856.

Building, and at No. 212 Clay Street. Before the end of the year and as late as 1860 his "music store" is listed under the name of "Atwill, Jos. F., & Co., 172 Washington Street."

While in New York, Atwill issued popular songs and instrumental pieces, many of which have fine pictorial covers which are excellent specimens of the lithographer's art in America. One example of these is "Broadway Sights," a song written and "sung with great applause by W. H. Latham," in 1835. A picture of Atwill's store at No. 201 Broadway, three doors from Fulton Street where the Telephone Building stands today, with a view of Broadway and St. Paul's Church are on the cover. (See: plate 29). One of his San Francisco imprints is very interesting historically. It is marked: "The First Piece of Music Pubd. in Cala." The title-page reads: "The California Pioneers, a Song respectfully inscribed to Mrs. J. Emerson Sweetser. Words and Music by Dr. M. A. Richter. Published & Sold by Atwill & Co. in San Francisco." This song was copyrighted in the U. S. District Court of California, March 19, 1852 and has a title cover lithographed by Quirot & Co. of San Francisco, depicting two pioneers, one on horseback and the other on foot, with California scenery in the background. An Atwill & Co. sheet-song publication, "El Eco Del Pacifico," by Jacques Coo, pictures the "music store" at No. 172 Washington Street. It was issued in 1853 and entered the same year.

The arranger of the Atwill collection was Francis H. Brown, a versatile song- and dance-music composer who flourished in the forties and fifties. A number of his compositions were published with highly colored title-pages and are collected today rather for their appeal to the eye than for their musical value. The Plume, Pride, Woodbird Polkas and others picturing gorgeously colored birds, have reappeared on modern lampshades.

Brown was also the author of a few didactic pieces of writing such as *The Pupils Primer* (Ditson, Boston, n.d.) which went through several editions. His portrait, reproduced here, appeared on the title-page of "I'll Love Thee in the Spring Time," one of his songs published in 1856 by William Hall & Son of New York.

This whole collection of patriotic songs, including Brown's arrangement of "The Star Spangled Banner" was published in pamphlet form by James G. Gregory, New York, 1861, with illustrations by F. O. C. Darley.

[1844]   No. 16

No separate title-page.

THE STAR-SPANGLED BANNER | National Song | written during the Bombardment of Fort McHenry | Baltimore, by the late | FRANCIS S. KEY ESQR. | Baltimore. Published by F. D. Benteen.

No date.   Plate number 418.

This Carr-type publication, of which music and text fill two unpaged inside pages, is copied from the Cole edition (No. 7). It answers the description of No. 7 in

[99]

every detail except in the text. Here, besides the misplaced word "was" in line 6 of the first stanza and the omission of "broad" in line 3 of the same stanza, "they'd" is substituted for "shall" in line 3 of third stanza. This reads: "A home and a country they'd leave us no more," and is the variation introduced by Atwill. (See: No. 15.)

The plate number appears in lower margins of pages [1] and [2].

The year 1844 is fixed for this edition by its plate number 418 since "Good-Bye" by J. C. Engelbrecht, plate number 409, and "Love Not, Quick Step" by James M. Deems, plate number 423, were both copyrighted by Benteen in 1844.

No. 16a

A variation of this edition appeared printed on two separate pages.

In 1839 Frederick D. Benteen purchased the stock and catalogue of John Cole and became the owner of the business at No. 137 Baltimore Street (Market Street). He remained at Cole's old premises until about 1848, when he removed to No. 181 Baltimore Street. Among his noteworthy publications are a number of Stephen C. Foster's songs. In the early fifties W. C. Miller and J. R. Beacham entered the firm as partners, changing the name to Benteen & Co. In 1853 it became Miller & Beacham.

Benteen, after selling to Miller & Beacham, still continued in the music trade. He is listed in Baltimore city directories for the next ten years as dealer and publisher doing business from his home. It is not certain whether Frederick D. Benteen, Jr., who was schooled in his father's business, was affiliated with him during these years. Both father and son died in the same month and year; F. D. Benteen, Jr. on the 2nd, and the elder Benteen on the 22nd of January, 1864.

[1844–1848]   No. 17

No separate title-page.

Collective title: YANKEE DOODLE | & | STAR SPANGLED BANNER. | Philadelphia, J. C. SMITH, 215 Chesnut St.

Plate number 623.

No date.

This Carr-type edition is a single-sheet issue, and with "Yankee Doodle" appears on two unpaged inside pages. It is printed from the same plates as the Osbourn edition (No. 12) plate number 128, and is identical with it except that here the publisher's imprint has been added in the caption title and the plate number is changed to 623. The serial number of "Yankee Doodle," which was the same as that of the "Star Spangled Banner" in the Osbourn issue, has been changed to 620 in this re-issue.

The caption title on page [2] reads: "STAR SPANGLED BANNER | Published by J. C. Smith, Phila."

Judging by the evidence of the plate number, this edition is not a direct reprint from the Osbourn plate, but a reprint made 'by another Philadelphia publisher who substituted his own plate number for Osbourn's and presently sold either the actual plate or the sheet-song to Jonathan C. Smith. Smith must have altered the imprint or merely added his name to it. He used no plate numbers of his own. There are entries in the records of the Copyright Office of the Library of Congress for the period April 1, 1845, to October 9, 1851. The actual deposits on file there (and most of the publications are on file), are without plate numbers.

Jonathan C. Smith began business in 1840 at No. 169 Chestnut Street, and in 1842 and 1843 was at No. 264 Chestnut Street. He acquired a great deal of music and some plates from such Philadelphia publishing houses as Fiot, Meignen & Co. and L. Meignen & Co. In 1844 Smith removed next door to 215 Chestnut Street, where, until 1839, Fiot, Meignen & Co., and L. Meignen & Co., consecutively, were in business. He remained there until 1848 and during this period re-issued a number of the latter firm's publications, changing their imprint to conform with his but retaining the old plate numbers. Serial numbers on copyrighted issues of Fiot, Meignen & Co. place their number 623 (the number on this issue) in 1838, and the corresponding numbers for L. Meignen & Co. in 1839 or thereabouts.

All the evidence thus points to the theory that Smith bought the "Star Spangled Banner" issue from Ld. Meignen & Co., who probably acquired it from Fiot, Meignen & Co. Their imprints are identical, and comparison of the sheets· yields even further corroborative data. Smith's name in the imprint line does not fit the space exactly; the word "Chestnut" continues to be mis-spelled "Chesnut"; and in the street address the numeral "7" has obviously been altered to read "5."

Smith published this piece between 1844 and 1848. From 1849 to 1853 he conducted business from No. 184 Chestnut Street, and for the next five years at No. 162. In 1859 his name disappears from city records. (See Addenda, page 216.)

[1845]   No. 18

No separate title-page.

THE STAR-SPANGLED BANNER | National Song | Written during the Bombardment of Fort McHenry | Baltimore, by the late | FRANCIS S. KEY ESQR. | Baltimore Published by J. E. Boswell.

———————

No   date.   Plate number 92.

This Carr-type edition, of which music and text fill two unpaged inside pages is a Cole adaptation. It is copied from the Benteen edition (No. 16) and in script and general appearance is a perfect imitation of it.

The text is the same as in No. 16.

The plate number appears in lower margins of pages [1] and [2].

This edition has been dated by checking the plate numbers on other copyrighted publications of this Baltimore dealer and publisher.

James E. Boswell, who first appears in city directories in 1842 as James Boswell, dealer in musical instruments and music publisher at the S.W. corner of Baltimore and Charles Streets, continued shifting addresses in Baltimore Street until the middle of the fifties, after which his name disappears from the records. In 1845, under the name of James E. Boswell, he is listed at No. 141 Baltimore Street; in 1847 at No. 219 and No. 112; and from 1848 to 1855 at No. 112. An advertisement in 1853 lists him at No. 223 Baltimore Street, which may have been his house address.

[1845–1851]   No. 19

No separate title-page.

THE | Star Spangled Banner. | NEW YORK Published at MILLETS MUSIC
   SALOON 329 Broadway.

No date.

This Carr-type publication is identical with the Geib edition (No. 3) and apparently copied from it.

Music and text fill two unpaged inside pages.

In the music the Bacon and Geib misprint "G" instead of "F" in the second bar of the introduction, is copied, and repeated in the seventh, or the second bar of the melody.

The text is the same as that of Geib's imprint, which was copied from the original Carr edition. All New York issues, the Geib, Hewitt & Jaques, and Millet editions, are noteworthy for being the only Carr-type editions which carry the original version without misplacement, curtailment or substitution.

William E. Millet never marked his music with plate numbers. His imprint with street address is of no assistance therefore in establishing a date for this edition, because city directories list him at No. 329 Broadway from 1839 to 1860. This is too wide a range of date to be of assistance in the chronology of undated publications.

The writer has in his collection a copy of this (Star Spangled Banner) imprint which bears the inscription: "Fillmore—Executive Mansion—Washington, D. C.—1851." This is sufficient proof that the piece was certainly not issued any later.

The general appearance and typography of the publication have all the characteristics of American music printing in the thirties. It is perfectly possible that Millet, who from 1836 to 1838 was at No. 375 Broadway, issued the song during this period with the above address in the imprint line and altered it later on when in 1839 he moved to No. 329 Broadway. If an old bound volume of sheet-music

[102]

which has come under the writer's observation is to be trusted, the song was in circulation before 1845. "The Star Spangled Banner" is included in this collection and the latest date of any of the other pieces, the majority of which were copyrighted, is 1845.

The firm of Millet, New York music publishers and dealers, was in business under various firm names and at various Broadway addresses from 1835 to 1879.

[1847–1851]   No. 20

No separate title-page.

THE STAR SPANGLED BANNER. | BOSTON: Published by E. H. WADE 197 Washington St.

No date.

This Carr-type edition of which music and text fill two inside pages is an exact copy of the C. Bradlee publication (No. 9.) printed from the same plates with the original publisher's imprint line changed to that of E. H. Wade.

Eben H. Wade, originally in the umbrella business, was for a number of years in partnership with John Ashton, Jr. under the firm name of John Ashton & Co. The combination of umbrella-making with music dealing, blend with a peculiar Boston flavor, and may have originated with the elder John Ashton, who went into the umbrella business in 1820. In 1825 he added music and musical instruments to his stock in trade and advertised them rather cleverly. In the writer's collection there is a print of that period engraved by Sparrow depicting an amusing scene in Olympus where the "jolly" gods are visited by a short rotund mortal who offers them "Sheet Music for Sale." The advertisement beneath reads:

"JOHN ASHTON. IMPORTER & MANUFACTURER of Musical instruments of every description and all other articles usually found in Music Stores. Also published by G. GRAUPNER Music Books for Piano forte, Clarionet, Hautboy Flute & Flageolet, with a great assortment, Songs, Duetts Waltzes Sonatas, Dances, Battles, Ovetures, [sic] &c &c. Pianofortes to hire. Instruments repaired and Timed. No. 197 Washington St. Boston."

In 1847 Wade went in for music-publishing on his own at No. 197 Washington Street. He probably bought some of C. Bradlee's stock, when the latter sold out to Ditson in 1846. At any rate, Wade acquired the "Star Spangled Banner" plates, which he republished during his short lived publishing venture. Oliver Ditson took over his stock and good will in 1851.

[103]

No separate title-page.

THE STAR SPANGLED BANNER | Written by | F. S. KEY ESQ. | AR-RANGED WITH AN ACCOMPANIMENT | FOR THE | PIANO FORTE. | BOSTON Published by OLIVER DITSON 115 Washington St.

No date.   Plate number 1473.

With the exception of a few minor changes and the addition of a right hand piano accompaniment this publication follows very closely the Carr arrangement (No. 4).

Music and text fill one outside and two inside pages 1–3.

The music is in 6/4 time in the key of C major. The flute arrangement is omitted. No arranger's name is given.

The text carries the misplaced word "was" in line 6 of first stanza, and in line 3 in the third verse the word "they'd" is given instead of "shall."

The publisher's plate number appears on the right hand corners in lower margins of pages 1–3. Verso of page 3 is blank.

This is the earliest Ditson issue of "The Star Spangled Banner" and was published at No. 115 Washington Street, Boston, in 1848. While there is no copyright or other date on the publication itself, its plate number is sufficient to place its date of appearance in that year. C. H. Granger's "Charlie's Quick Step," which bears plate number 1454, was copyrighted and published in 1848. Edward L. White's "In The Lonely Grove I Linger," plate number 1530, was also issued in the same year. It is obvious, therefore, that the "The Star Spangled Banner" edition with plate number 1473 is of the same vintage.

(This publication was reprinted in "The Masonic Harp; George W. Chase, K. T. Boston: Oliver Ditson & Co., 1858 pp. 134, 135.").

The house of Oliver Ditson is one of the oldest as well as the largest music concerns in this country.

Oliver Ditson (1811–1888) started in the music trade at the age of twelve by entering the employ of Samuel H. Parker, a Boston book and music dealer, who establish himself in business in 1811. They formed a partnership in 1836 which lasted until 1842, when Ditson bought out the senior partner and became the sole owner.

From 1844 to 1857 Oliver Ditson occupied No. 115 Washington Street, Boston. In the following year, admitting John C. Hayes as a partner, he formed the firm of Oliver Ditson & Co., and removed to the newly erected building at No. 277 Washington Street. During the next fifty years or so the business kept growing and the firm, as it expanded, changed its location several times. It now occupies a large building at Tremont Street.

[104]

THE STAR SPANGLED BANNER
Published by Oliver Ditson, Boston.
Page [1]. *(Bib. No. 21.)*

THE STAR SPANGLED BANNER
Published by Oliver Ditson, Boston.
Page [2]. *(Bib. No. 21.)*

2

On the shore dimly seen thro' the mists of the deep,
Where the foe's haughty host in dread silence reposes.
What is that which the breeze, o'er the towering steep
As it fitfully blows half conceals half discloses;
Now it catches the gleam of the morning's first beam,
In full glory reflected now shines in the stream;
'Tis the star spangled banner. O! long may it wave,
O'er the land of the free, and the home of the brave.

3

And where is that band who so vauntingly swore,
'Mid the havoc of war and the battle's confusion,
A home and a country they'd leave us no more,
Their blood hath wash'd out their foul footsteps pollution
No refuge could save the hireling and slave,
From the terror of flight or the gloom of the grave:
And the star spangled banner in triumph doth wave,
O'er the land of the free, and the home of the brave.

4

O thus be it ever when freemen shall stand,
Between their loved home, and the wars desolation,
Blest with victory and peace, may the heaven rescued land,
Praise the power that hath made and preserved us a nation.
Then conquer we must, for our cause it is just,
And this be our motto "In God is our trust;"
And the star spangled banner in triumph shall wave,
O'er the land of the free, and the home of the brave.

THE STAR SPANGLED BANNER
Published by Oliver Ditson, Boston.
Page [3]. (Bib. No. 21.)

OLIVER DITSON
Drawn from a Photograph by Max Jacobs.

Collective title-page.

COLLECTION OF NATIONAL SONGS OF AMERICA. | No. 5. | THE STAR SPANGLED BANNER." | The Words written by | FRANCIS S. KEYS, ESQ. | (OF BALTIMORE.) The Symphonies and Accompaniments | Composed & Arranged | AND RESPECTFULLY INSCRIBED | TO | the Officers of the Army and Navy | OF THE | UNITED STATES, | by | FRANCIS H. BROWN. |

No.

1. LAND OF WASHINGTON!	Price	4. HUZZA! HUZZA!
2. HAIL COLUMBIA!	25 Cts. ea.	5. STAR SPANGLED BANNER!
3. OUR FLAG IS THERE!	Nett.	6. YANKEE DOODLE!

NEW YORK. | Published by JOLLIE, 300, Broadway |

Entered according to Act of Congress AD 1843 by Jos. F. Atwill in the Clerks Office of the District Court of the Southern Dist. of New York.

———

Copyrighted.

No. 5 ["]THE STAR SPANGLED BANNER"—This edition is a republication of the Atwill edition (No. 15), and is printed from the same plates.

The collective title-page is the same as in No. 15 except that in the majority of copies Atwill's name is omitted at the top of the page and Jollie's name and address substituted in the publisher's imprint line. Key's name is spelled "Keys." Atwill's copyright notice appears in the lower margin of the title-page, verso of which is blank.

Music and text fill three unpaged inside pages and tally with Atwill's edition in every respect.

No. 22a

An issue of this edition appeared without the collective title-page described above but with the same pictorial cover used by Atwill for the publication of the series of six songs in collective form. (See: No. 15a.)

Slight changes in the cover were made by Jollie. His name appears at the top and also in the imprint line, which gives the No. 300 Broadway address. The engraver here is: "Ackerman. Lith 329 Broadway."

Atwill's copyright notice (1843) is printed in the lower margin of the cover-title, verso of which is blank.

No copy of this Jollie issue of "The Star Spangled Banner" has come under the writer's observation. The description in this collation was made from a copy which

THE STAR SPANGLED BANNER
Published by Jollie, New York.
Title-page. (Bib. No. 22a.)

bears plate number 8612, pagination 3–5, and an extra line following the "Note by the Publisher" in the caption title on page 3.

It is an established fact that Jollie and Atwill never used plate numbers. Examination of hundreds of their publications reveal no such marks.

This copy is from Jollie's stock which was taken over by Oliver Ditson in 1855. Before disposing of this stock, the Boston publisher had added his plate number, the pagination and the extra line. There are a number of these copies extant, the writer knows at least three of them. The next year Ditson reprinted the song from the Jollie plates in an edition of his own with his own copyright notice and a newly designed cover (see: No. 29).

The verso of page 5 of this variation helps to establish the approximate date of the Jollie issue. The full page is used for the advertisement of "Samuel Jollie, Publisher of Music, And Manufacturer of Musical Instruments, 300 Broadway, New York." Mention is made herein of his purchase of Atwill's stock, and his recent acquisition of the entire Stock of Music, with the extensive Catalogue of Dubois & Warriner, late Dubois & Stodart. At the bottom of the page is the following announcement: "Dubois & Warriner, Late Dubois & Stodart, Beg to inform their friends and the public that they have disposed of their Catalogue of Music to Samuel C. Jollie, and have removed their Stock of Piano Fortes to the new and elegant Warerooms, 300 Broadway, where will be found a complete assortment of PIANO FORTES."

Dubois & Warriner are listed under that firm name in New York city directories for 1850 at No. 315 Broadway, and for 1851 and 1852 at No. 300 Broadway. In 1853 the business was still conducted from the latter address, but is recorded under the name of William Dubois. In the following year the firm disappeared.

Jollie, no doubt, published his collection of national songs after 1849 when he succeeded Atwill and before 1852, since he acquired the catalogue of Dubois & Warriner in 1851.

Samuel C. Jollie, the most prominent of three brothers who followed the music trade in New York, began his career in about 1838. In 1849 he bought out Joseph F. Atwill's store and remained at No. 300 Broadway until 1854. In 1855 he removed to No. 519 Broadway and before the end of the year discontinued business. His catalogue was taken over by Oliver Ditson of Boston.

[1851]   No. 23

No separate title-page.

THE | STAR SPANGLED BANNER. | Reduced Price | 8 Cents | NEW YORK
Published by Wm. HALL & SON, 239 Broadway.

———————

No date.   Plate number 1427.

The music and text of this Carr-type edition which fills two unpaged inside pages is printed from the same plates as the edition published by Hewitt & Jaques (No.

11). It is identically the same except that the notation "Reduced Price 8 Cents" is added here.

The plate number appears in the lower margins of pages [3] and [4].

Fortunately the house of William Hall & Son furnished their publications with plate numbers through which the date of this edition has been established.

The New York firm of William Hall & Son came into existence in 1847. At that time William Hall, who had been part owner with John Firth of the house of Firth & Hall, withdrew and taking his son, James F. Hall, into partnership, opened his own store at No. 239 Broadway. This enterprising concern is listed at the above address from 1848 until 1858. From 1859 to 1870 it appears at No. 543 Broadway. Finally James F. Hall left to join the army. The elder Hall continued in business until 1873, the time of his death. The firm was eventually absorbed by Oliver Ditson & Co.

[1851]   No. 24

No separate title-page.

THE | STAR SPANGLED BANNER | A Popular | NATIONAL AIR, | Arranged with an Accompaniment for the | Piano Forte. | New York, Firth, Pond & Co. 1 Franklin Square.

————

No date.   Plate number 1426.

This publication is a re-issue of the Firth & Hall edition No. 8, and is printed from the same plates. The publisher's imprint has been changed to that of Firth, Pond & Co., and a plate number has been added. This number appears in the lower margins of page [1]–3. The numeral "3" is found on the bottom of page [1], and pages 2 and 3 bear the notation "Star Spangle 3."

The date of this publication has been established by checking the corresponding plate numbers on Firth, Pond & Co. copyrighted publications.

No. 24a

Copies of this edition carry neither the plate number, the numeral, nor the notation as described above.

1852   No. 25

STAR-SPANGLED BANNER.

St. Louis, Mo. Published by J. L. Peters & Bro.
Entered according to Act of Congress in the year 1852 by J. L. Peters & Bro. in the Clerk's Office of the Eastern District Court of Missouri.

————

Copyrighted.   Plate number 1812.3.
[112]

STAR SPANGLED BANNER
Published by Oliver Ditson & Co., Boston.
(Reissue from J. L. Peters & Bro., St. Louis Edition.)
Title-page. (Bib. No. 25a.)

STAR SPANGLED BANNER
Published by Oliver Ditson & Co., Boston.
(Reissue from J. L. Peters & Bro., St. Louis Edition.)
Page [3]. (Bib. No. 25a.)

STAR SPANGLED BANNER

Published by Oliver Ditson & Co., Boston.

(Reissue from J. L. Peters & Bro., St. Louis Edition.)

Page [4]. *(Bib. No. 25a.)*

free and the home of the brave.

free and the home of the brave.

free and the home of the brave.

free and the home of the brave.

2

On the shore dimly seen, thro' the mist of the deep,
Where the foe's haughty host in dread silence reposes,
What is that which the breeze, o'er the towering steep,
As it fitfully blows, half conceals, half discloses?
Now it catches the gleam of the morning's first beam,
In full glory reflected, now shines in the stream:
'Tis the star-spangled banner — Oh! long may it wave
O'er the land of the free and the home of the brave.

3

And where is that band who so vauntingly swore,
'Mid the havoc of war and the battle's confusion,
A home and a country they'd leave us no more?
Their blood has wash'd out their foul footsteps' pollution;
No refuge could save the hireling and slave,
From the terror of flight, or the gloom of the grave,
And the star-spangled banner in triumph doth wave
O'er the land of the free and the home of the brave.

4

Oh! thus be it ever, when freemen shall stand
Between their loved home and the war's desolation;
Blest with vict'ry and peace, may the heav'n rescued land
Praise the Power that hath made and preserved us a nation.
Then conquer we must, when our cause it is just,
And this be our motto, "In God is our trust,"
And the star-spangled banner in triumph shall wave
O'er the land of the free and the home of the brave.

Star Spangled Banner. 1812 3

STAR SPANGLED BANNER
Published by Oliver Ditson & Co., Boston.
(Reissue from J. L. Peters & Bro., St. Louis Edition.)
Page [5]. *(Bib. No. 25a.)*

No copy of this edition has been available, therefore, it has been collated from a republication of it issued by Oliver Ditson & Co., Boston. (No. 25a.)

No. 25a.

The collective title-page of this Boston reprint bears a lithographed scene depicting Columbia holding a large American flag with people of all nations gathered around it and the Capitol and Washington Monument showing in the background. This title-page with its list of popular national songs and instrumental pieces reads:

No. 25a

COLUMBIA | A COLLECTION |
OF AMERICAN | NATIONAL | MELODIES. |

VOCAL

Columbia's Flag is waving a welcome	E. DE BARRY	30
One hundred years ago	W. S. HAYS	30
Marching 'neath our Starry Flag	H. GLOVER	30
E Pluribus Unum	PENDLETON	40
Ark of our Union	PENDLETON	40
QUARTET		
Our Banner of Glory	PETERS	50
Brave Boys are they	WORK	30
QUARTET		
American Ensign	WEBSTER	50
Brave men behold our fallen chief	WEBSTER	50
CENT'Nl. QT.		
Let the hills and vales resound	RICHARDS	12
Hail Columbia	BARKER	30
Star Spangled Banner	MERKLEY	30
Yankee Doodle	BARKER	30
Stand by the Flag of our Nation	HASTINGS	30
QUARTET		
E Pluribus Unum	PENDLETON	40

INSTRUMENTAL

Old 76	MEDLEY OF AIRS	RAPHAELSON	60
New 76	MEDLEY OF AIRS	RAPHAELSON	60
Medley of all Nations		DRESSLER	75
Grand National Medley		PATTIANI	60
New Union Medley		KINKEL	40
Columbia's Flag	MARCH	DE BARRY	35
Ark of our Union	VAR.	BELLAK	50
E Pluribus Unum	VAR.	GROBE	60
Hail Columbia	VAR.	BELLAK	50
Washington's March	VAR.	BELLAK	50
Yankee Doodle	VAR.	BELLAK	50
Star Spangled Banner		BEYER	35
Brave boys are they	VAR.	GROBE	75
Hail Columbia	EASY	DRESSLER	25

BOSTON. | Published by OLIVER DITSON & CO. 451 Washington St. |

NEW YORK. SAVANNAH GA. BALTIMORE MD. CINCINNATI. SAN FRANCISCO. PHILA.
C. H. DITSON & CO. LUDDEN & BATES. OTTO SUTRO. GEO. D. NEWHALL & CO. SHERMAN CLAY & CO. J. E. DITSON & CO.

CHICAGO. ST. LOUIS.
LYON & HEALY. J. L. PETERS. |

J. H. BUFFORDS SONS LITH BOSTON & NEW YORK.

Pages 3–5, which bear the music and text, are the original edition, as published by J. L. Peters & Bro., St. Louis, Mo.

The caption title on page 3 reads: "STAR-SPANGLED BANNER. | Arranged as a SONG with CHORUS by C. Merkley." The publishers' copyright notice appears in the lower margin of page 3.

The music is an arrangement for voice with chorus for four voices and piano accompaniment in 3/4 time in the key of C major.

The word "broad" in line 3 of the first stanza of the text was omitted. Line 3 of the third verse reads: "A home and a country they'd leave us no more," the variation introduced by Atwill in No. 15.

The publishers' plate number (1812.3) appears in lower margins of pages 3–5; pages 4 and 5 bear the notation, "Star Spangled Banner," and a star. Verso of page 5 is blank.

Judging by the illustrated cover and the series of patriotic numbers listed thereon, this undated Boston republication was probably issued in 1877, in commemoration of the Philadelphia Centennial Exposition held the year before. Corroborating data are found on the imprint, where the names of J. E. Ditson & Co., Philadelphia and J. L. Peters, St. Louis are added to that of Oliver Ditson & Co., Boston. The Ditson branch was established in Philadelphia in 1875, and the Peters firm was absorbed by Oliver Ditson & Co., in 1877.

[1853]   No. 26

ENGLISH EDITION.

Separate title-page.

THE STAR SPANGLED BANNER. | National American Song. | Sung by Mr. White, | in his | Lectures on American Minstrelsy. | Written by | J. F. KEY, ESQR. . | (OF WASHINGTON.) | The Symphonies & Accompaniments, | Composed by | E. J. LODER. | Ent. Sta. Hall.—Pr | 2/ — | LONDON, | D'ALMAINE & CO. 20, SOHO SQUARE.

No date.   Plate number 8635.

The engraved title-page of this English edition is ornamented with a cut of the American flag which shows thirteen stars in its union. The author's name appears as "J. F. Key." Verso of title-page is blank.

Music and text fill pages 1–5.

The caption title on page 1 reads: "The Star Spangled Banner."

The music, an arrangement for voice and piano accompaniment in 6/8 time in the key of C major, is an adaptation of the original tune of "To Anacreon in Heaven." It differs from the American version in that it has "F natural" instead of "F sharp," which Thomas Carr used.

All four verses including the much discussed third verse are the same as in the

THE STAR SPANGLED BANNER
Published by D'Almaine & Co., London.
Title-page. (Bib. No. 26.)

DR ARNE.
PURCELL.
SHIELD.
DIBDIN.
DR MACKAY.

H. RUSSELL.
J.P. KNIGHT.
A. LEE.
DAVY.
CARTER.

Admired

SONGS & BALLADS

WITH

PIANO-FORTE ACCOMPANIMENTS,

By the best

COMPOSERS

WHITAKER.
STORACE.
CORRI.
J.R. THOMAS.
S.C. FOSTER.
W.H. MONTGOMERY.
T. MOORE.
BRAHAM.
C. HORN.
REEVE.
DEMPSTER.

THE

STAR SPANGLED BANNER,

AND

HAIL! COLUMBIA,

AMERICAN NATIONAL SONGS.

POPULAR ENGLISH SONGS AND BALLADS.

Published in the MUSICAL BOUQUET Single N.º 3.ª Double N.ºª 6.ᵈ each
* The figures before each song refer to its number in the Musical Bouquet.

90, THE WOLF.
177, THE LADS OF THE VILLAGE.
500, THE FRIAR OF ORDERS GREY.
706, THE FINE OLD ENGLISH GENTLEMAN.
2189, THE BATTLE OF THE NILE.
3083, TOM STARBOARD.
3106, THE SAPLING OAK.
3114, THE SPIRIT OF THE STORM.
3143, REST, WARRIOR, REST.
3237, TELL HER I'LL LOVE HER.
3274, UNDER THE GREENWOOD TREE.

138, DOWN AMONG THE DEAD MEN.
190, WAPPING OLD STAIRS.
594, POOR JOE THE MARINE.
765, COME IF YOU DARE.
2882, FLOW, THOU REGAL PURPLE STREAM.
3095&6, MAD TOM SCENA.
3107, ON BY THE SPUR OF VALOUR GOADED.
3128, JOLLY YOUNG WATERMAN.
3208&9, FRIEND OF THE BRAVE.
3246, CHERRY RIPE.
3288, SMILE AGAIN MY BONNIE LASSIE.

157, STAND TO YOUR GUNS.
203, SALLY IN OUR ALLEY.
611, BLACK-EYED SUSAN.
2026, HEARTS OF OAK (WITH CHORUS).
2887, THE RIGHT END OF LIFE.
3105, MY FRIEND IS THE MAN.
3113, IN THE DOWNHILL OF LIFE.
3131, SANDY AND JENNY.
3210&11, THE SOLDIER'S DREAM.
3264, GLASSES SPARKLE ON THE BOARD.
3291, THE LASS OF RICHMOND HILL.

LONDON.

PUBLISHED BY C. SHEARD, MUSICAL BOUQUET OFFICE, 192, HIGH HOLBORN.

CITY WHOLESALE AGENTS. E.W. ALLEN, 11, AVE MARIA LANE, AND F. PITMAN, 20, PATERNOSTER ROW.

N.º 2445, MUSICAL BOUQUET

THE STAR SPANGLED BANNER
Published by C. Sheard; The Musical Bouquet Office, London.
Title-page. (Bib. No. 26a.)

Key manuscript and line 3 of the first stanza reads: "A home and a country should leave us no more."

The plate number and the notation "The Star-spangled banner" appear in the lower margins of pages 1–5. Verso of page 5 bears an advertisement which supplies the date of the publication. It reads: "Tariff No. 2, September 1853," and advertises for sale: "Harmoniums, of D'Almaine & Co., 20, Soho Square, London."

The arranger of this interesting edition, Edward J. Loder (1813–1865), was a well-known English musician and composer of opera who wrote an enormous number of single songs and ballads, among the most popular of which are "The Brave Old Oak," "Old House at Home," "The Last Links are broken," and "O Speed my Bark."

The White, mentioned on the title-page, may have been William White, the minstrel, a member of the "Ethiopian Serenaders" who gave concerts in England and made a tremendous hit with their "black-face" performances.

No. 26a

Another undated English edition of the song, a *Musical Bouquet* issue, was entered for copyright at Stationer's Hall, London, on December 5, 1874, according to information furnished by Mr. C. B. Oldman, the librarian of the Department of Printed Books at the British Museum.

The collective title-page of this edition, (see: plate No. 36) lists a number of favorite British vocal pieces. The names of the composers who made these songs famous appear in the upper half of the page on scrolls which wind around a circle. A few names of American song writers are among them. The plate number—2445—appears in the left hand corner in the lower margin of the title-page.

Music and text of "The Star Spangled Banner" fill verso of title-page (page 2) and the upper part of page 3; the lower halves of pages 3 and 4 bear "Hail Columbia." The caption title on page 2 reads: "THE STAR-SPANGLED BANNER. | Sung by "THE OLD FOLKS", Mrs. HOWARD PAUL &c."

The music is an easy waltz-like arrangement for voice with piano accompaniment in 6/8 time in the key of B flat major. The melody version is that of Thomas Carr. No arranger's name is given.

The text is practically the same as the original broadside, except that line 5 of the last stanza reads: "Then conquer we must, when our cause is so just" instead of "Then conquer we must, if our cause it is just." The third verse is omitted.[16]

---

[16] This stanza with its bitter denunciation of the English is obsolete today. It is present in the various sheet-music issues described in this bibliography, but it has long been excluded from songbook versions. The Oliver Ditson Company of Boston banned it as early as 1857 when they printed the song in their *Golden Wreath,* "choice collection of favorite melodies arranged by L. O. Emerson."

Separate title-page.

NATIONAL SONG | STAR | SPANGLED BANNER | Written during the Bombardment of Fort McHenry | (BALTIMORE) | by the late | FRANCIS S. KEY Esq. | Published by MILLER & BEACHAM Baltimore | Successors to F. D. Benteen | F. McCarthy [engr.]

Entered according to Act of Congress in the Year 1855 by Miller & Beacham in the Clerks Office of the District Court of Md.

————————

Copyrighted.   Plate number 2845.

The engraved title-page is ornamented with a large shield, which holds the title including the imprint. The lower part of it is surrounded by a branch of laurel and acorn. The American flag, liberty pole and cap, spears and Roman fasces are grouped around the shield. The copyright notice appears in the lower margin of the title-page, verso of which is blank.

Music and text fill pages 3–5. The caption title on page 3 reads: "Star-Spangled Banner | NATIONAL SONG."

The music is a simple arrangement for voice and piano accompaniment of waltz-like nature in 3/4 time in the key of B flat major. No arranger's name is given.

The word "was" in line 6 of first stanza in the text is placed correctly, but the word "broad" in line 3 of the same stanza is omitted. Line 3 of the third verse reads: "A home and a country shall leave us no more."

The plate number appears in the lower margins of pages 3–5, and the name "Webb" is printed in the right hand lower corner of page 5. Verso of page 5 is blank.

No. 27a.

A variant of No. 27 appeared with the numerals "2½" [within star] printed in the lower half of the title-page.

William C. Miller and Joseph R. Beacham who had been partners since 1850 with F. D. Benteen under the firm name of Benteen & Co. at No. 181 Baltimore Street, became the successors of Benteen either in 1853 or early in 1854. The new firm continued in business as Miller & Beacham at No. 10 North Charles Street until 1864. In the following year Beacham disappears from city records, but Miller carried on alone at the above address until 1872. In 1873 Oliver Ditson & Co. took over his catalogue with what remained of the Benteen & Co. music and plates and the old John Cole stock.

STAR SPANGLED BANNER
Published by William Hall & Son, New York.
Title-page. (Bib. No. 30.)

THE WILLIAM HALL & SON BUILDING, NO. 239 BROADWAY, NEW YORK.
(By Courtesy of the Fridenberg Galleries)

Collective title-page.

NATIONAL SONGS | OF | AMERICA. | ARRANGED FOR THE | PIANO FORTE | BY | FRANCIS H. BROWN. |

2½ [within star]
Land of Washington
Hail Columbia
Our Flag is there

J. H. Bufford's Lith |
Huzza! Huzza! Columbia
Star Spangled Banner
Yankee Doodle

BOSTON | Published by OLIVER DITSON 115 Washington St. |

S. T. GORDON   J. E. GOULD   C. C. CLAPP & CO.   D. A. TRUAX
N. York   Phila.   Boston   Cinn.

Entered according to Act of Congress in the Year 1856 by O. Ditson in the Clerks Office of the District Court of Mass.

Copyrighted.   Plate number 8612.

Like the Jollie issue (No. 22) this edition is another reprint from the original Atwill plates (No. 15.). Oliver Ditson acquired these plates from Samuel C. Jollie, whose stock and catalogue he took over in 1855. In 1856 he recopyrighted and re-published the whole collection of "National Songs" furnishing the set with a new collective title-page.

The title-page is lithographed with scenes and figures from American history. It is in plain black and also appears with the illustrations printed on a brown background. The publisher's copyright notice appears in the lower margin of the title-page, verso of which is blank.

The music and text, which fill pages 3–5 are identical with the Atwill and Jollie publications except that the caption title on page 3 of this republication has an additional line at the conclusion of the "Note by the Publisher" which reads: "Written by Frances S. Keys"—with the two misspellings in Key's name. The plate number appears in the lower right hand corners of pages 3–5. Verso of page 5 is blank.

Worthy of special note in connection with this edition is the fact that the lithographed cover, which appeared on all six songs in the set, is the work of Winslow Homer and bears his initials "W.H."

Homer, who was to become one of our country's greatest artists, went to work for J. H. Bufford, the Boston lithographer, in 1855 and during his three years there made a number of lithographed title-pages all published by Oliver Ditson. The writer knows of about a dozen examples of these and there are probably more. These lithographs are doubly interesting because Homer executed them between the ages of nineteen and twenty-one. They constitute, therefore, some of the earliest work of this master, and possibly the first artistic work for which he received remuneration.

[126]

NATIONAL SONGS
OF
AMERICA,

ARRANGED FOR THE
PIANO FORTE
BY
FRANCIS H BROWN.

Land of Washington   Huzza! Huzza! Columbia
Hail Columbia   Star Spangled Banner
Our flag is there   Yankee Doodle

BOSTON
Published by OLIVER DITSON 115 Washington St.

S.T.GORDON   J.E.GOULD   C.C.CLAPP&CO   D.A.TRUAX
N.York   Phila   Boston   Cinn

Entered according to Act of Congress in the Year 1856 by O.Ditson in the Clerks Office of the District Court of Mass.

THE STAR SPANGLED BANNER
Published by Oliver Ditson, Boston.
Title-page. (Bib. No. 29.)

STAR SPANGLED BANNER
Published by Oliver Ditson, Boston.
Page [3]. *(Bib. No. 29.)*

Collective title-page.

NATIONAL SONGS OF AMERICA | ARRANGED WITH ACCOMPANI-
MENT FOR THE PIANO FORTE | By | Wm. DRESSLER. |
J. C. Pearson, N. Y. [engr.]—2½ [within star]—No. [3.]
NO. 1. YANKEE DOODLE. NO. 2. HAIL COLUMBIA. |
NO. 3. STAR SPANGLED BANNER. |

NEW YORK | Published by WILLIAM HALL & SON, 239 Broadway.

No date.   Plate number 3470.

The engraved title-page is ornamented with thirteen stars, which form a circle
around the word "NATIONAL." Verso of title-page is blank.

Music and text fill pages 3–5.

The caption title on page 3 reads: "THE STAR SPANGLED BANNER. |
AMERICAN NATIONAL SONGS. | Arranged by Wm DRESSLER. | No. 3."

The music is an arrangement for single voice and a chorus for four voices with
piano accompaniment, in 6/4 time in the key of B flat major.

The text is that used by Carr.

The plate number appears in lower margins of pages 3–5. Lower margin of page
5 bears the notation: "In the absence of a Choir, the Air or Soprano may be sung
with Accompaniment." Verso of page 5 is blank.

The date of this edition has been fixed by comparison of plate numbers found
on copyrighted pieces issued by the publishers.

No. 30a

In 1859, when William Hall & Son moved their place of business to No. 543
Broadway, where they remained until 1870, they reissued this set of *National Songs
of America,* with the imprint on the title-page changed to read: "543 Broadway."

William Dressler, whose arrangement of "The Star Spangled Banner" became
popular was used extensively in the late fifties and early sixties, wrote a number of
vocal and instrumental pieces for William Hall & Son while he was their proof-reader
and musical editor, was born in England of German parents. He first came to America
in the early fifties after completing his musical education in Germany. He toured with
Ole Bull as his accompanist, and as solo pianist, and for a few years traveled with
concert companies. Finally he settled in New York and devoted himself to the work
of church organist. Dressler wrote some fine church music and also popular songs,
and made instrumental arrangements. His services as an all around musician, teacher
and conductor were much in demand. He died in New York in 1914, in his eighty-
eighth year.

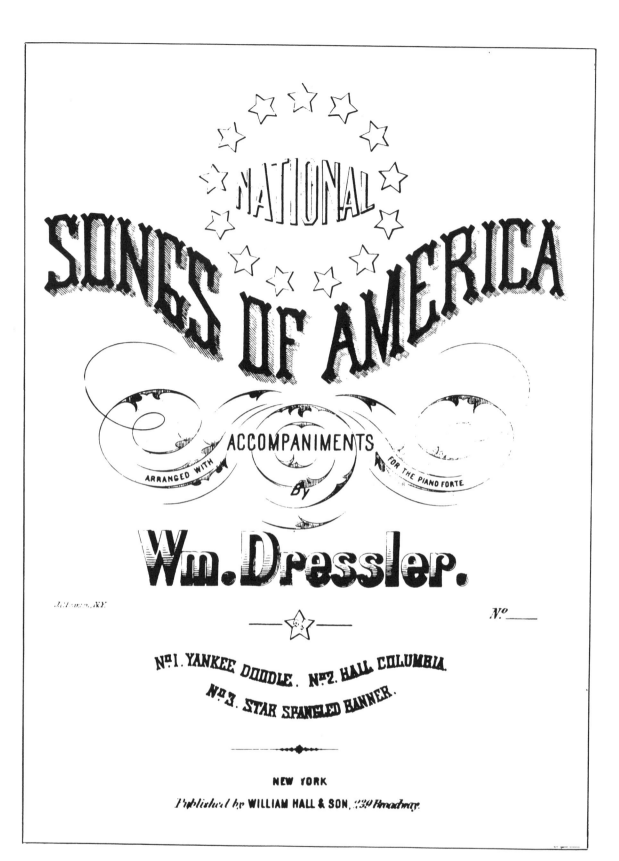

STAR SPANGLED BANNER
Published by William Hall & Son, New York.
Title-page. (Bib. No. 30.)

THE STAR SPANGLED BANNER.

AMERICAN NATIONAL SONGS.
No. 3.

Arranged by W^M DRESSLER.

Maestoso.

1. O say can you see by the dawn's ear-ly light, What so
2. On the shore dim - ly seen thro' the mists of the deep, Where the

proudly we hail'd at the twilight's last gleaming Whose broad stripes and bright stars thro' the
foe's haughty host in dread silence re - po - ses, What is that which the breeze, o'er the

pe - rilous fight, O'er the ramparts we watch'd were so gallantly streaming; And the
to - wering steep, As it fit - ful - ly blows, half con - ceals, half dis - clo - ses; Now it

STAR SPANGLED BANNER
Published by William Hall & Son, New York.
Page [3]. (Bib. No. 30.)

3.

And where is that band, who so vauntingly swore
  That the havoc of war and the battle's confusion
A home and a country, shall leave us no more,
  Their blood has wash'd out their foul footsteps polution;
No refuge could save the hireling and slave,
From the terror of flight or the gloom of the grave
  And the star spangled banner, in triumph shall wave,
  O'er the land of the free, and the home of the brave.

4.

O! thus be it ever when freemen shall stand,
  Between their lov'd home and the war's desolation,
Blest with victory and peace, may the heaven rescued land
  Praise the Pow'r that has made and preserv'd us a nation.
Then conquer we must, when our cause it is just,
And this be our motto, In God is our trust;
  And the star spangled banner in triumph shall wave,
  O'er the land of the free, and the home of the brave.

STAR SPANGLED BANNER
Published by William Hall & Son, New York.
Page [4]. *(Bib. No. 30.)*

CHORUS.

Soprano. 1. O say does that star spangled banner yet wave O'er the land of the free and the home of the brave?

Tenor. 2. 'Tis the star spangled banner, O! long may it wave, O'er the land of the free and the home of the brave?

In the absence of a full Chorus, the Air or Soprano may be sung with Accompaniment.

3470

STAR SPANGLED BANNER
Published by William Hall & Son, New York.
Page [5]. *(Bib. No. 30.)*

Collective title-page.

AMERICAN | NATIONAL SONGS | ARRANGED WITH ACCOMPANI-
MENTS FOR THE PIANO FORTE. | 2½ [within star] |
SHALL THE UNION BE DISSOLVED?   OUR FLAG IS THERE. |
STAR SPANGLED BANNER.   E PLURIBUS UNUM. |
HAIL COLUMBIA.   YANKEE DOODLE. |

PUBLISHED | Cincinnati. W. C. PETERS & SONS—PETERS, CRAGG & CO.,
Louisville. |
         New York   St. Louis.
    WM. HALL & SON.   BALMER & WEBER. |

Entered according to Act of Congress in the year 1856, by W. C. Peters & Sons,
in the Clerk's Office of the Southern District Court of Ohio.

Copyrighted.   Plate number 1398.

The engraved title-page is ornamented at the top with thirteen stars, forming a
half-circle over the heading "AMERICAN NATIONAL SONGS." Verso of title-
page is blank.

Music and text fill pages 3–5. The caption title on page 3 reads: "STAR-
SPANGLED BANNER. | Arranged as a SONG with CHORUS by C. Merkley."

The copyright notice is printed in lower margin of page 3.

The plate number appears in lower margins of pages 3–5; pages 4 and 5 bear the
notation: "Star Spangled Banner." Verso of page 5 is blank.

Music and text of this edition is identical with the J. L. Peters, St. Louis
publication, (No. 25a), and printed from the same plates. The publishers, W. C.
Peters & Sons, substituted their plate number and omitted the small star which
precedes the notation, "Star Spangled Banner" in lower margins of pages 4 and 5
in the earlier edition.

No. 31a

A variant of this edition appeared with the song "ARK OF OUR UNION" replacing the song listed on the title-page, "E PLURIBUS UNUM." (A copy of this
imprint is in the Malcolm N. Stone collection, West Englewood, N. J.)

No. 31b

Still another variant exists with a seventh number, "MARSEILLES HYMN,"
added to the list of songs printed on the same title-page.

(A copy of this variant was examined by the writer in a music book belonging
to a private family in New York City.)

[134]

AMERICAN

National Songs

ARRANGED WITH ACCOMPANIMENTS FOR THE

PIANO FORTE.

SHALL THE UNION BE DISSOLVED?

STAR SPANGLED BANNER.

HAIL COLUMBIA.

OUR FLAG IS THERE.

E PLURIBUS UNUM.

YANKEE DOODLE.

PUBLISHED

Cincinnati. W. C. PETERS & SONS — PETERS. CRAGG & CO. Louisville.

New York
WM. HALL & SON.

St. Louis
BALMER & WEBER.

STAR SPANGLED BANNER
Published by A. C. Peters & Sons, Cincinnati.
Title-page. (Bib. No. 31.)

No. 31c

Collective title-page.

MUSIC For The UNION |

E Pluribus Unum...............Song...... .35	Our Flag is There......	.35
E Pluribus Unum.............Quartette.. .35	Ark of our Union......	.35
Stand by the Flag of the Nation............ .35	Flag of our Union......	.35
The Flag with Thirty-four Stars............ .35	I'm Going to Fight mit Sigel......	.30
Strike while the Iron is hot............... .35	Battle Prayer......	.30
Watch-Tower of Freedom................ .50	The Picket......	.35
Our Banner of Glory...........Quartette.. .40	On to the Field where Glory calls us......	.40
Never shall the Union be dissolved......... .35	Hail Columbia......	.30
When the lonely Watch I'm keeping........ .30	Star-Spangled Banner......	.30
Our Flag's the Flag of Washington......... .35	Yankee Doodle......	.30
Battle Chorus; or, Charge, Boys, Charge!... .35	Marseillaise Hymn......	.30

[star]

Cincinnati. A. C. Peters & Bro. 69 West 4th St. |

Entered according to Act of Congress in the year 1864 by A. C. Peters & Bro., in the Clerk's Office of the District Court of the U. S. for the Southern District of Ohio.

Copyrighted.

Plate number 1398.

MUSIC for the UNION

E Pluribus Unum	Song	35
E Pluribus Unum	Quartette	35
Stand by the Flag of the Nation		35
The Flag with Thirty-four Stars		35
Strike while the Iron is hot		35
Watch-Tower of Freedom		50
Our Banner of Glory	Quartette	40
Never shall the Union be dissolved		35
When the Lonely Watch I'm keeping		30
Our Flag's the Flag of Washington		35
Battle Chorus; or, Charge, Boys, Charge!		35

Our Flag is There	35
Ark of Our Union	35
Flag of Our Union	35
I'm Going to Fight mit Sigel	30
Battle Prayer	30
The Picket	35
On to the Field where Glory calls us	40
Hail Columbia	30
Star-Spangled Banner	30
Yankee Doodle	30
Marseillaise Hymn	30

Cincinnati. A.C.Peters & Bro. 69 West 4th.St.

Entered according to Act of Congress, in the year 1864 by A. C. Peters & Bro., in the Clerk's Office of the District Court of the U. S. for the Southern District of Ohio.

STAR SPANGLED BANNER
Published by A. C. Peters & Bro., Cincinnati.
Title-page. (Bib. No. 31c.)

TITLE-PAGE OF "HIGHLANDERS' MARCH"
Published by A. C. & J. L. Peters, Cincinnati, 1860. Showing the A. C. & J. L. Peters Music
Store in Cincinnati.
(By Courtesy of Miss Edith A. Wright, Washington, D. C.)

This publication is a reissue of No. 31 and was printed from the same plates, except for the title-page.

The color-lithographed title cover shows a liberty cap and a large American flag with thirty-four stars in its union. The title: "MUSIC For THE UNION" is profusely designed and printed in colors. The A. C. Peters & Bro. copyright notice appears in lower margin of title-page, verso of which is blank. The original copyright notice of W. C. Peters & Sons is printed in lower margin of page 3; their plate number (1398) appears in lower margins of pages 3–5, and pages 4 and 5 bear the notation: "Star Spangled Banner." Verso of page 5 is blank.

No. 31d

A republication of No. 31c, printed from the same plates with the title-page somewhat changed, was issued in 1866 by J. L. Peters & Bro. of St. Louis.

The title-page has the same cover design as No. 31c with the following alterations: the two columns of vocal numbers on the lower half of the page have been divided into "VOCAL" and "INSTRUMENTAL" series: the A. C. Peters & Bro. imprint was made to read: "St. Louis, Mo. J. L. Peters & Bro. 49 North Fifth Street," and the copyright notice in the lower margin, which reads: "Entered . . . in the year 1866 by J. L. Peters & Bro. . . ." was substituted for that of A. C. Peters & Bro.

(A copy of this edition has been reported to the writer by a Philadelphia collector.)

Attention must be drawn to the fact that these publications, (Nos. 31, 31a, 31b and 31c), were originally issued by J. L. Peters & Bro., St. Louis, 1852. (See: No. 25a). Examination of other patriotic numbers, such as "Hail Columbia" and "Yankee Doodle," (listed in No. 25a), indicate that the St. Louis publisher sold the plates of these to W. C. Peters & Sons. They afterwards passed to A. C. Peters & Bro., and each of these publishers issued them with their own imprint and copyright notice. In 1866, however, when J. L. Peters & Bro. bought out W. C. Peters and his successors, they once more became the owners of this set of national songs. In 1877 they were acquired by Oliver Ditson & Co. of Boston.

The founder of the family of Peters, American music publishers, William Cumming Peters (1806–1866), a composer and a fine pianist and violinist, emigrated from England in the early 1820's. He taught music in Pittsburgh from 1825 to 1828 and opened the first regular piano store in town. In the following year he moved to Louisville, Kentucky, where he began business as a publisher. In 1839 he established a branch in Cincinnati and ten years later another branch in Baltimore. In all three places, the firm went under the names of W. C. Peters and W. C. Peters & Co., but subsequently changed to Peters & Field, Peters, Field & Co., and W. C. Peters & Sons in Cincinnati; and to Peters & Webb and Peters, Cragg & Co., in Louisville. In 1856 the latter branch was bought out by Tripp of Louisville who continued in business under the name of Tripp & Cragg. A view of their store is shown on the title-page of a "collection of songs" published by the firm in 1858.

W. C. Peters, who is said to be the original arranger and distributor of T. D.

[139]

Rice's "Jim Crow," was also affiliated with Stephen C. Foster, whose early songs he published between 1846 and 1850.

About 1864 Peters retired and the firm was succeeded by that of A. C. Peters & Bro., of No. 69 West Fourth Street, Cincinnati, evidently the sons of the above. Their activities ceased in 1866 when the rival house of J. L. Peters & Bro., of St. Louis absorbed them.

Whether John L. Peters was a member of the same family is not known, nor is much information concerning A. C. Peters available. They were apparently in business together for at least a year or so. In 1860 a number of publications appeared with the imprint: "Cincinnati, Published by A. C. Peters & J. L. Peters, No. 94 West Fourth Street," and with their names given in the copyright notice line. One of the issues, "The Highlanders' March. Arranged for, and dedicated to the Highland Guards by W. C. Peters," is furnished with color-lithographed title-page picturing a group of Highlanders with three of the members prominently portrayed in front of A. C. & J. L. Peters' music store in Cincinnati.

The firm of J. L. Peters & Bro. is listed in St. Louis, Mo., at least as early as 1852 and up to 1866, the year it was removed to New York.

[1857]   No. 32

Collective title-page.

NATIONAL SONGS. |

STAR SPANGLED BANNER.   LA MARSEILLAISE. |
YANKEE DOODLE.   HAIL COLUMBIA. |

SUNG BY |
MADLLE T. PARODI. |

Single 2½ [within star]   7½ [within star] Complete |

Philadelphia R. WITTIG, No. 148 Arch Street |

L. N. Rosenthal, Lith. Phila.

———————

No date.   Plate number R. W. 30.

This edition displays a kind of colored music cover that flourished in the sixties of the last century and appeared on national song collections, both vocal and instrumental, issued by different publishers. It featured the American flag and flags of other nations. Our national emblem is displayed singly, in pairs and in fours, and is pictured frequently with the tricolor of Republican France. The inclusion of "La Marseillaise" as one of the songs listed on the title pages explains this apparent anachronism.

The covers are an early specimen of chromo-lithography, a process of color-printing first used for this purpose by L. N. Rosenthal of Philadelphia who lithographed several music titles in the fifties. Rosenthal's method was followed by T. S. Sinclair, P. S. Duval, J. H. Bufford and other lithographers, who produced a quantity of these collective title covers for national song collections.

NATIONAL SONGS.

STAR SPANGLED BANNER
YANKEE DOODLE

LA MARSEILLAISE
HAIL COLUMBIA.

SUNG BY

MAD.lle T. PARODI.

Single

Complete

Philadelphia R WITTIG, N.º 146 Arch Street

L.N Rosenthal, Lith Phil.ª

STAR SPANGLED BANNER
Published by R. Wittig, Philadelphia.
Title-page. (Bib. No. 32.)

THE STAR SPANGLED BANNER.

AMERICAN NATIONAL HYMN.

STAR SPANGLED BANNER
Published by R. Wittig, Philadelphia.
Page [3]. (Bib. No. 32.)

STAR SPANGLED BANNER
Published by R. Wittig, Philadelphia.
Page [4]. *(Bib. No. 32.)*

STAR SPANGLED BANNER
Published by R. Wittig, Philadelphia.
Page [5]. *(Bib. No. 32.)*

The title-page of this edition of "The Star Spangled Banner" depicts the American and French Republican flags crossed. The American flag shows a constellation of thirteen stars. Verso of title-page is blank.

Teresa Parodi whose name is featured on the cover, was a famous Italian singer, brought to America in 1851 by the impresario Maretzek in order to stem the Jenny Lind furore which was raging then. She toured the country in 1851 and 1852 and delighted her audiences with her rendition of patriotic songs. Her portrait, a lithograph by Sarony & Major, N. Y., was published in 1851 by Wm. Hall & Son of New York and appears on the title-page of "I greet thee gentle flowers," an air from "Giovanna di Napoli" by Maurice Strakosh.

Music and text fill pages 3–5. The caption title on page 3 reads: "The STAR SPANGLED BANNER. | A NATIONAL SONG."

Although the arranger's name is not given, the music is unquestionably one of the arrangements made by William Dressler for Wm. Hall & Son. (See: No. 30.)

It was used subsequently by other publishers.

The text is the same as in No. 30.

The plate number appears in lower margins of pages 3–5. Verso of page 5 bears Wittig's advertisement of publications issued from his store at No. 148 Arch Street.

Rudolph Wittig, of whom little is known, had a varied career in Philadelphia. City directories list him from 1856 to 1868 as music dealer, teacher, lager beer and restaurant keeper, clerk and publisher at ever changing street addresses. In 1857 he appears at No. 148 Arch Street, where he acquired the music and plates of George Vogt.

Vogt was a piano maker by trade and is recorded under that heading at various addresses in 1852 and as late as 1862. From 1855 to 1857 his residence and store was located at No. 148 Arch Street. It was during his stay here that he engaged in the music publishing business. His imprints invariably bear that address and his copyrights show the years 1855 and 1856 as date of deposit. Vogt was primarily a piano manufacturer and his publishing venture seems to have been either unprofitable or to have made too heavy demands on his time. Before the end of 1856 he sold his plates and catalogue. That the purchaser was Rudolph Wittig is evident from the advertisement on verso of page 5 already mentioned where all of Vogt's publications are listed in addition to his own. "The Star Spangled Banner" issue is one of the latter. For some reason or other, his publications are scarce. The writer has seen very few of them, and these, though they bear the imprint "R. Wittig; No. 148 Arch Street," never carry a copyright notice.

At the close of 1857 Wittig sold out to Lee & Walker, who subsequently re-issued the latter's publications with Vogt's copyright notice and Wittig's plate marks under their own imprint line. (See: No. 36.)

(The collation of this imprint was made from a copy examined by the writer in a collection of music owned by Mr. Constantine Weikert of Englewood, N. J. Copies of "Yankee Doodle," with plate mark "R. W. 16," and "The Marseilles Hymn," with plate mark "R. W. 37" of the songs listed on the above title-page are in the same collection. Both imprints bear Wittig's advertisement on verso of last page as mentioned above.)

Collective title-page.

AMERICAN NATIONAL SONGS: |
HAIL COLUMBIA— |YANKEE DOODLE— |
STAR SPANGLED BANNER. | COMPOSED FOR THE | Piano. |
Guitar 2½ [within star]   Piano 2½ [within star] |

Philadelphia LEE & WALKER 188 Chestnut St. |

T. Sinclair's lith. Phila.

——————

No date.   Plate number 5884.3.

The title-page is lithographed in color, showing a pair of crossed American flags with thirteen stars in each union.

Music and text fill pages 3–5. The caption title on page 3 reads: "THE STAR SPANGLED BANNER."

The music, the arranger's name of which is not given, is an easy arrangement for voice and piano in 3/4 time in the key of C major.

The text is the same as Carr's except that in line 3 of the first stanza "Whose broad stripes and bright stars . ." the word "broad" has been omitted.

The plate number appears in lower margins of pages 3–5. Verso of page 5 is blank.

It is by means of the plate number that this edition has been dated.

Lee & Walker, a prominent firm of Philadelphia music publishers, was founded by Julius Lee (died 1875) and William Walker (died 1857). Both had been in the employ of George Willig (Senior) of Philadelphia for a number of years In 1845 they started in business for themselves and opened a store at No. 120 Walnut Street, where they remained until 1848. From 1849 to 1851 they were at No. 162 Chestnut Street. The firm continued at shifting addresses on Chestnut Street until 1875, when Oliver Ditson & Co. bought them out. In 1852 they were listed at No. 188, and sometime during 1857 moved to larger quarters at No. 722 Chestnut Street, having, in the meantime, acquired the stock and catalogue of George Willig of Philadelphia, who died in 1851.

Lee & Walker, according to plate numbers on copyrighted issues published the set of *American National Songs,* which includes "The Star Spangled Banner" (plate number 5884.3) in 1857. The earliest publication issued from No. 188 Chestnut Street on record in the files at the Library of Congress, "Kossuth Grand Reception March" by William Fischer, has plate number 4226 and was copyrighted in 1852. Later publications from No. 188 Chestnut Street, Nos. 1 and 2 in "Beauties of Beethoven" by Charles Grobe, are both copyrighted in 1857 and bear plate numbers 5876 and 5911 respectively.

[146]

AMERICAN NATIONAL SONGS:

HAIL COLUMBIA_
YANKEE DOODLE_
STAR SPANGLED BANNER.

COMPOSED FOR THE

Guitar

Piano.

Piano

Philadelphia LEE & WALKER, 188 Chestnut S!

STAR SPANGLED BANNER
Published by Lee & Walker, Philadelphia.
Title-page. (Bib. No. 33.)

THE STAR SPANGLED BANNER.

STAR SPANGLED BANNER
Published by Lee & Walker, Philadelphia.
Page [3]. *(Bib. No. 33.)*

STAR SPANGLED BANNER
Published by Lee & Walker, Philadelphia.
Page [4]. (Bib. No. 33.)

Home of the Brave.

2

On the shore dimly seen thro' the mists of the deep,
Where the foe's haughty host in dread silence reposes;
What is that which the breeze, o'er the towering steep
As it fitfully blows, half conceals, half discloses;
Now it catches the gleam of the morning's first beam,
In full glory reflected, now shines in the stream ——
Tis the Star Spangled Banner, Oh! long may it wave,
O'er the Land of the Free, and the Home of the Brave.

3

And where is that band who so vauntingly swore,
That the havoc of war and the battle's confusion
A home and a country shall leave us no more ——
Their blood has washed out their foul footstep's polution
No refuge could save the hireling and slave,
From the terror of flight, or the gloom of the grave;
And the Star Spangled Banner in triumph doth wave,
O'er the Land of the Free and the Home of the Brave.

4

Oh thus be it ever when Freemen shall stand,
Between their Loved Home, and the wars desolation;
Blest with victory and peace, may the Heaven rescued land,
Praise the Power that hath made and preserved us a Nation:
Then conquer we must, when our cause it is just,
And this be our motto —"In God is Our Trust!"
And the Star Spangled Banner in triumph shall wave,
O'er the Land of the Free and the Home of the Brave.

STAR SPANGLED BANNER
Published by Lee & Walker, Philadelphia.
Page [5]. (Bib. No. 33.)

Collective title-page.

AMERICAN NATIONAL SONGS: |
HAIL COLUMBIA— | YANKEE DOODLE— |
STAR SPANGLED BANNER. | COMPOSED FOR THE | Piano. |
Guitar 2½ [within star]   Piano 2½ [within star]

Philadelphia LEE & WALKER 722 Chestnut St.

No date.   Plate number 5884.3.

This publication is a reissue of No. 33 and printed from the same plates. The title-page only was changed; a set of larger American flags in color with each union showing thirty stars was substituted. The lithographer's name was omitted and the imprint changed from No. 188 Chestnut Street to No. 722.

Judging by the new title cover, this republication appeared between 1858 and 1860. Lee & Walker altered their imprint line in 1858 after moving to No. 722 Chestnut Street, and after 1860 employed a somewhat different title-page for their national song publications.

AMERICAN NATIONAL SONGS:

HAIL COLUMBIA

YANKEE DOODLE.

STAR SPANGLED BANNER.

COMPOSED FOR THE

Piano.

LEE & WALKER

STAR SPANGLED BANNER
Published by Lee & Walker, Philadelphia.
Title-page. (Bib. No. 33a.)

Collective title-page.

Flowers OF THE SOUTH | A Collection of favorite | Songs and Ballads | Arranged for the | GUITAR | by | T. Brigham Bishop. |

BEAUTIFUL BLUE VIOLETS

BLIND GIRL
BY THE SAD SEA WAVES
CALL ME THINE OWN
CARRIER DOVE
EVER OF THEE
HAS SORROW THY YOUNG
    DAYS SHADED

HOME OF MY HEART
I FORGET THE GAY WORLD
YANKEE DOODLE

I HAVE SOMETHING SWEET TO
    TELL YOU |
I WANDERED BY THE BROOKSIDE |
LITTLE GIPSY JANE |
LITTLE WHITE COTTAGE |
NOT FOR GOLD OR PRECIOUS
    STONES |
OLD MOUNTAIN TREE |
O WHISTLE AND I'LL COME TO
    YOU |
SAY WHAT SHALL MY SONG BE |
STAR SPANGLED BANNER |
WHAT'S A THE STEER KIMMER |

2½ [within star]

BOSTON | Published by OLIVER DITSON & Co 277 Washington St |

C. C. CLAPP & CO. BECK & LAWTON. TRUAX & BALDWIN. S. T. GORDON.
   Boston   Philadelphia   Cincinnati   N. York

No date.   Plate number 19099.

Verso of ornamental title-page blank.

Music and text fill pages 3–5. The caption title on page 3 reads: "THE STAR SPANGLED BANNER. | Happy Thoughts." The plate number appears in the right hand corners on lower margins of pages 3–5. Verso of page 5 is blank.

The music is an arrangement for voice with guitar accompaniment in 6/4 time in the key of C major.

The text is that introduced by Atwill in 1843. (See: No. 15).

The year 1858 has been fixed as the time when this edition appeared in circulation, by comparison of plate numbers on copyrighted Ditson publications. The publication "Castles in the Air—Scotch Song," with a Ditson imprint, copyright notice of 1858 and plate number 19119 proves this date beyond a doubt.

T. Brigham Bishop, the composer of this set of guitar pieces, was one of the group of American song writers who flourished in the middle of last century, and whose songs and ballads were widely sung and very popular.

His likeness appears on the title-page of one of his songs, "Nellie Dear Lies Sleeping," a publication issued in 1857 by Higgins Brothers, of Chicago.

[153]

[1858]

Collective title-page.

[154]

THE | VOCALIST | A COLLECTION OF
Trios, Quartettes, Choruses etc. |

Title	Type	Composer	No.
GIVE ME A CUP	Trio		4
ANNIE LAURIE	"		22
BRAGELA		STEVENS	7
CANADIAN BOAT SONG	"	MOORE	2
CAPTIVE TO HIS BIRD	"	MAZZINGHI	2
COME FAIRIES TRIP IT O'ER THE GRASS	"	PARRY	5
FRIEND WE COME	"	ORPHEUS	2
HALLELUJAH CHORUS (MESSIAH)	Quartette	HANDEL	2
HARK! APOLLO STRIKES THE LYRE	Quartette	BISHOP	5
MALTESE BOATMANS SONG	Trio	DEVERAUX	2
PHANTOM SHIP	"	BISHOP	2
BLOW GENTLE WINDS	"	"	2½
WINDS WHISTLE COLD	"	"	5
TO GREECE WE GIVE OUR SHINING BLADES	"	"	2
FORESTERS SOUND THE CHEERFUL	Quartette	"	5
YES! 'TIS THE INDIAN DRUM	"	"	2½
AWAY THE MORNING FRESHLY	"	MASANIELLO	3½
LITTLE FARM WELL TILLED	Trio	PARRY	2
RODERICH VICH ALPINE		MAZZINGHI	5
YE SHEPHERDS TELL ME	"		3
SHIP AHOY	Quartette	WEBB	2
HUNTING CHORUS		DER FREISCHUTZ	2
FAIR HARVARD			2½
AWAKE! AEOLIAN LYRE			2½
HAIL SMILING MORN		SPOFFORTH	
HAIL TO THE CHIEF			1½
STAR SPANGLED BANNER			2½

Title	Type	Composer	No.
MARYLAND CADETS GLEE.	Quartette	ALPINE	2
SOUND THE LOUD TIMBREL (MARIAM'S SONG)	"	PUCITTA	2
MY SWEET DORABELLA	Trio	MOZART	5
STRIKE THE CYMBALS	Solo & Quartette	PUCITTA	2
THE TIGER CROUCHES IN THE WOOD	"	BISHOP	5
O STRANGER LEND THY GENTLE BARK	Trio	STEVENSON	2½
HARK THE CONVENT BELLS ARE RINGING	"	"	2
THE LIGHT CIGAR		DEVERAUX	2½
OUR BOAT SITS LIGHTLY			2½
FRIENDS WE COME WITH HEARTS OF GLADNESS			2½
BARK BEFORE THE GALE		WILLIS	5
CROWS IN THE CORNFIELD	Quartette	PHILLIPS	2½
HARK! THE CURFEW	"	ATWOOD	5
LITTLE PIGS	"	LEE	1½
SLEEP ON	"	HERMANN	3
HUNTSMAN'S MORNING GLEE	"	BRICHER	2½
LUTZOW'S WILD HUNT	"	VON WEBER	2
PRAYER—HEAR O KIND & GRACIOUS	"	ROSSINI	2½
SEE OUR OARS	"	STEVENSON	2½
SEE OUR BARK	Trio	"	2½
DAYBEAM IS O'ER THE SEA			2½
ST. PAUL'S ADVICE TO TIMOTHY	"	ZELTER	2½
THE OLD TIMEPIECE ON THE STAIRS	"		1½
WILD OLD WOODS	Quartette		2½

C. C. CLAPP & CO.
Boston

BOSTON | Published by OLIVER DITSON & CO Washington St |
BECK & LAWTON.
Philada.

TRUAX & BALDWIN.
Cincinnati

S. T. GORDON.
N. York

This edition, with the exception of a few slight changes, is the same as the Wm. Hall & Son issue (No. 28) and evidently copied from it.

Music and text are printed on verso of title-page (page 2) and on pages 3–5. The caption title on page 2 reads: "THE STAR SPANGLED BANNER. | FOR FOUR VOICES. | The Vocalist."

In the music the quarter note "C" in the first bar of the melody and in the first bar of the chorus as given in No. 28, has been altered into two eighth notes.

The text, however, which is the same as in No. 28, is differently arranged. Instead of verses two, three and four appearing on page 5, the four stanzas are inter-lined with the music on pages 2–5.

The plate number appears in the right hand corners on lower margins of pages 2–5. Verso of page 5 is blank.

Corresponding plate numbers on copyrighted Oliver Ditson & Co. publications of that period indicate that this undated edition was published in 1858. (See: No. 34.)

THE

VOCALIST

A COLLECTION OF

Trios, Quartetts, Choruses, etc.

GIVE ME A CUP			4	STAR SPANGLED BANNER	2¼
ANNIE LAURIE	Trio		2	MARYLAND CADETS GLEE	Quartett. ALPINE 2
BRAGELA	"	STEVENS	7	SOUND THE LOUD TIMBREL Miriams Song	" PUCITTA 2
CANADIAN BOAT SONG	"	MOORE	2	MY SWEET DORABELLA	Trio MOZART 5
CAPTIVE TO HIS BIRD	"	MAZZINGHI	2	STRIKE THE CYMBALS Solo & Quartett.	PUCITTA 2
COME FAIRIES TRIP IT O'ER THE GRASS	"	PARRY	5	THE TIGER CROUCHES IN THE WOOD	" BISHOP 5
FRIENDS WE COME	Quartett.	ORPHEUS	2	O STRANGER LEND THY GENTLE BARK	Trio STEVENSON 2½
HALLELUJAH CHORUS Messiah		HANDEL	2	HARK THE CONVENT BELLS ARE RINGING	" " 2
HARK! APPOLLO STRIKES THE LYRE	Quartett.	BISHOP	5	THE LIGHT CIGAR	DEVERAUX 2½
MALTESE BOATMANS SONG	& Trio	DEVERAUX	2	OUR BOAT SITS LIGHTLY	2½
PHANTOM SHIP	"	BISHOP	2	FRIENDS WE COME WITH HEARTS OF GLADNESS	2½
BLOW GENTLE GALES	"	"	2½	BARK BEFORE THE GALE	Quartette WILLIS 5
WINDS WHISTLE COLD	"	"	5	CROWS IN THE CORNFIELD	" PHILLIPS 2½
TO GREECE WE GIVE OUR SHINING BLADES	"		2	HARK! THE CURFEW	" ATWOOD 5
FORESTERS SOUND THE CHEERFUL	Quartette	"	5	LITTLE PIGS	" LEE 1½
YES! TIS THE INDIAN DRUM	" "	"	2½	SLEEP ON	" HERMANN 3
AWAY THE MORNING FRESHLY	" MASANIELLO		3½	HUNTSMAN'S MORNING GLEE	" BRICHER 2½
LITTLE FARM WELL TILLED	Trio	PARRY	2	LUTZOW'S WILD HUNT	" VON WEBER 2
RODERICH VICH ALPINE		MAZZINGHI	6	PRAYER - HEAR O KIND & GRACIOUS	" ROSSINI 2½
YE SHEPHERDS TELL ME		"	3	SEE OUR OARS	" STEVENSON 2½
SHIP AHOY	Quartette	WEBB	2	SEE OUR BARK	Trio " 2½
HUNTING CHORUS	DER FREYSCHUTZ		2	DAYBEAM IS O'ER THE SEA	" " 2½
FAIR HARVARD			2½	ST. PAUL'S ADVICE TO TIMOTHY	ZELTER 2½
AWAKE! AEOLIAN LYRE			2½	THE OLD TIMEPIECE ON THE STAIRS	1½
HAIL SMILING MORN		SPOFFORTH		WILD OLD WOODS	Quartette 2½
HAIL TO THE CHIEF					

BOSTON

Published by OLIVER DITSON & Co. Washington St

C. C. CLAPP & Co.	BECK & LAWTON	TRUAX & BALDWIN	S. T. GORDON
Boston	Phila.	Cincinnati	N York

STAR SPANGLED BANNER
Published by Oliver Ditson & Co., Boston.
Title-page. (Bib. No. 35.)

Collective title-page.

NATIONAL SONGS. |
STAR SPANGLED BANNER.   LA MARSEILLAISE. |
YANKEE DOODLE.   HAIL COLUMBIA. |
SUNG BY | MADLLE T. PARODI. |
Single 2½ [within star]   7½ [within star] Complete |

PUBLISHED BY LEE & WALKER 722 CHESTNUT ST | PHILADELPHIA

No date.   Plate number R. W. 30.

This publication is a reissue of the Wittig (No. 32) edition and printed from the same plates with the original plate number retained. The retouched title-page, which bears no lithographer's name, carries the new imprint line of Lee & Walker.

Music and text on pages 3–5 are absolutely the same as in No. 32. Verso of page 5 is blank.

In 1857 or early in 1858 Rudolph Wittig sold his stock and plates to Lee & Walker among which were the series of *National Songs*. These pieces were printed from the Wittig plates with the new imprint on the cover during the years 1858 and 1860. That this issue of "The Star Spangled Banner" appeared not later than 1860 is proven by a copy dated 1860 which came to the writer's notice.

[1861]   No. 36a

Collective title-page.

NATIONAL SONGS. |
STAR SPANGLED BANNER.   LA MARSEILLAISE. |
YANKEE DOODLE.   HAIL COLUMBIA. |
SUNG BY |
MADLLE T. PARODI. |

Philadelphia: LEE & WALKER, 722 Chestnut St.

No date.   Plate number R. W. 30.

This is a reissue of No. 36 and was published in 1861. It has a newly lithographed cover, set in different letter type and is ornamented with a pair of larger American flags which show thirty-four stars in each union. This design was adopted after Kansas joined the Union in March 1861, adding the thirty-fourth star.

Some copies of this edition appeared with different advertisements on verso of page 5. One copy gives a list of a series of pieces: *Buds and Blossoms* . . . . by Charles Grobe and the imprint and copyright notice of "Winner & Shuster; 1854."

TO M.ʳˢ AMELIA BLOOMER.

TITLE-PAGE OF THE "COSTUME POLKA", INSCRIBED TO MRS. AMELIA BLOOMER,
EARLY SUFFRAGIST AND DESIGNER OF THE BLOOMER COSTUME,
AND VIEW OF THE LEE & WALKER ESTABLISHMENT

Septimus Winner, who became widely known as the publisher of songs written under the pseudonym, Alice Hawthorne, started in business in Philadelphia in 1845. In 1854 Shuster became a partner and the firm was changed to Winner & Shuster. This partnership, however, was shortlived, for two years later Shuster withdrew and Winner was again sole proprietor. Part of the Winner & Shuster music and plates were sold in 1856 to Lee & Walker who reissued these pieces with their own imprint but retained the Winner & Shuster copyright notice.

Another copy which carries the Lee & Walker advertisement of *New Method for the Piano Forte* by Charles Grobe gives the publisher's address as No. 722 Chestnut Street, is dated 1859 but bears no copyright notice.

[1858–1860]   No. 37

Separate title-page.

Star Spangled Banner | SONG & CHORUS |
AND THE STAR SPANGLED BANNER IN TRIUMPH SHALL WAVE, | O'er
the land of the Free and the home of the Brave | 2½ [within star]

BUFFALO, | Published by BLODGETT & BRADFORD, 209 Main St. |

ROCHESTER	CLEVELAND,	NEW-YORK,
J. M. WILLSON.	S. BRAINARD & CO.	FIRTH, POND & CO.

No date.

The engraved title-page is embellished with a large American flag in color showing thirty stars. Verso of title-page is blank.

It is a curious fact that music covers picturing the flag during the period of 1858 to 1860 display only thirty stars in its union, which is officially incorrect. There should be a star for each state. In 1858 there were thirty-two states in the Union and the thirty-third (Oregon) was admitted in 1859. In 1861, when Kansas became a full fledged state, this error was rectified and the number of stars was changed to thirty-four.

Music and text of this Buffalo edition fill pages 3–5. The caption title on page 3 reads: "THE | STAR SPANGLED BANNER."

The music is an arrangement for voice and chorus for four voices with piano accompaniment in 3/4 time in the key of C major. No arranger's name is given.

The text is the same as that used by Carr.

The name of the engraver "Pearson" is printed in the lower right hand corner of page 5. Verso of page 5 is blank.

This publication was issued between 1858 and 1860. Several reissues of this edition, which have come to light, confirm this date. Descriptions of which follow.

Blodgett & Bradford, Buffalo music publishers, conducted business under this firm name only from 1858 to 1863. In 1864 J. R. Blodgett became the sole owner.

BUFFALO.
Published by BLODGETT & BRADFORD, 209 Main St.

ROCHESTER,
J M WILLSON

CLEVELAND,
S. BRAINARD & CO.

NEW-YORK,
FIRTH POND & CO

STAR SPANGLED BANNER
Published by Blodgett & Bradford, Buffalo.
Title-page. (Bib. No. 37.)

Separate title-page.

Star Spangled Banner | SONG & CHORUS |
AND THE STAR SPANGLED BANNER IN TRIUMPH SHALL WAVE, |
O'er the land of the Free and the home of the Brave | 2½ [within stars]

BUFFALO, | Published by BLODGETT & BRADFORD, 209 Main St. |

| ROCHESTER, | CLEVELAND, | NEW-YORK, |
| J. M. WILLSON. | S. BRAINARD & CO. | FIRTH, POND & CO. |

No date.

Except for a change in the title-page, this edition is a reissue of No. 37 printed from the same plates.

The four stars have been added to the constellation in the flag so that it shows thirty-four stars in its union. This design was adopted in 1861 after the state of Kansas became a member of the Union.

The name "PEARSON" in lower right hand corner of page 5 is omitted.

Separate title-page.

STAR SPANGLED BANNER | SONG & CHORUS | AND THE STAR
SPANGLED BANNER IN TRIUMPH SHALL WAVE, | O'er the land of
the Free and the home of the Brave | 2½ [within star]

BUFFALO, | Published by BLODGETT & BRADFORD, 209 Main St. |

| ROCHESTER, | CLEVELAND, | NEW-YORK, |
| J. P. SHAW. | S. BRAINARD & CO. | FIRTH, POND & CO. |

No date.

This edition is a reissue of 37a, printed from the same plates.

The title-page, however, has been partly re-engraved. The changes are as follows: The flagstaff has been ornamented with tassels; the title "STAR SPANGLED BANNER," is printed in capital roman letter type, replacing the old title which was printed in gothic script. In the new title the letters are composed of small stars and stripes in colors. The notation "SONG & CHORUS" is ornamented with scrolls and leaf design. In the imprint line the name of "J. P. Shaw," Rochester is substituted for that of "J. M. Willson," Rochester.

John M. Willson is listed in Rochester city directories for 1853 and 1854 as clerk at "No. 35 Edinburgh." He appears again in 1861 at the same address. Charles Willson, a music teacher, is recorded at this place at the same time. In 1863–1864 John M. Willson is listed as "Capt. 3d. Cavalry."

Joseph P. Shaw, at No. 104 State Street, Rochester's most important music seller and publisher, who carries a half advertisement in the directory for 1859, no doubt, acquired the agency for the Buffalo firm of Blodgett & Bradford in about 1861, after Willson joined the army.

This edition was published not later than 1862 and probably in 1861. Firth, Pond & Co., the New York house listed in the imprint, became Wm. A. Pond & Co., in January 1863, when John Firth left the old house and formed his own shortlived firm of Firth, Son & Co.

Blodgett & Bradford issued an edition of the "Star Spangled Banner" in instrumental form in 1861. The title-page which shows the same decorated title and flag design as in No. 37b, was changed to read: "STAR SPANGLED BANNER | TRANSCRIBED FOR THE PIANO | BY | Alfred H. Pease." The publisher's imprint, and the Rochester, Cleveland and New York publishers' names are the same as in No. 37b. The copyright notice and date 1861 appears in the lower margin of the title-page.

[1861–1862]   No. 37c

Collective title-page.

STAR SPANGLED BANNER | THE AMERICAN FLAG | SONG & CHORUS | AND THE STAR SPANGLED BANNER IN TRIUMPH SHALL WAVE, | O'er the land of the Free and the home of the Brave |

2½ [within star]

BUFFALO, | Published by BLODGETT & BRADFORD, 209 Main St. |

| ROCHESTER, | CLEVELAND | NEW YORK, |
| J. P. SHAW. | S. BRAINARD & CO. | FIRTH, POND & CO. |

No date.

Except for a collective title-page, this edition is absolutely the same as No. 37b.

"THE AMERICAN FLAG" which appears under the leading title was a new patriotic song with words by Prof. J. W. Lawton and music by J. M. Mills. The two songs listed were never published under one cover but appeared separately with this title-page. Why a collective title cover was used instead of a separate one for each song, is at present inexplicable.

(A copy of this edition has been reported to the writer as being in the possession of A. A. Bieber of Manasquan, N. J.)

STAR SPANGLED BANNER

THE AMERICAN FLAG

SONG & CHORUS

AND THE STAR SPANGLED BANNER IN TRIUMPH SHALL WAVE,
O'er the land of the Free and the home of the Brave

BUFFALO.
Published by **BLODGETT & BRADFORD,** 209 Main St

ROCHESTER,
J.P. SHAW

CLEVELAND
S.BRAINARD & CO.

NEW-YORK,
FIRTH POND & CO

STAR SPANGLED BANNER AND THE AMERICAN FLAG
Published by Blodgett & Bradford, Buffalo.
Title-page. (Bib. No. 37c.)

Separate title-page.

Star Spangled Banner | NATIONAL SONG | for the | Piano | written by Francis S. Key. | Gillingham. |

Published by GEORGE WILLIG Baltimore.

ENTERED ACCORDING TO ACT OF CONGRESS IN THE YEAR 1859 BY G. WILLIG IN THE CLERKS OFFICE OF THE DISTRICT COURT OF MD.

Copyrighted.   Plate number 2723.

The engraved title-page is elaborately ornamented with lines, clusters of leaves and flowers, and especially decorative letters for the title and the author's name. Verso of title-page blank.

Music and text fill pages 3–5.

The caption title on page 3 reads: "THE STAR SPANGLED BANNER. | NATIONAL SONG." The copyright notice appears in lower margin of page 3.

The music is an arrangement for voice and a chorus for four voices with piano accompaniment in 3/4 time in the key of C major. No arranger's name is given.

The text is that introduced in the Atwill (1843) edition (No. 15).

The plate number appears in lower margins of pages 3–5, and the name "French" is printed on the bottom of page 5. Verso of page 5 is blank.

This Baltimore edition, the fourth of "The Star Spangled Banner" issues published by the famous house of George Willig, is not copied from any of Carr's arrangements. Yet, in its simple musical treatment, it bears a faint resemblance to the Carr arrangement. It is written in the same key, and as a more striking similarity Carr's original coda, the final fanfare which was copied in many arrangements, has also been adopted in this edition. It is splendidly engraved throughout and a credit to American music typography.

(The collation of this edition has been made from a photostat in the Library of Congress.)

The Baltimore house of George Willig, founded about 1822 by George Willig Junior, carried on into the twentieth century. In 1868, shortly before the elder Willig retired, he took his two sons, Joseph E. and Henry Willig, into partnership, changing the firm name to George Willig & Co. He died in 1874, in his eighty-first year. Joseph E. Willig died in 1895, at the age of sixty-five, and Henry, the younger brother, who was born in 1835, continued in business until the time of his death in 1909. In the following year the old firm was taken over by the G. Fred Kranz Music Company of Baltimore.

No. 39

[1859–1860]

Collective title-page.

SONGS OF ALL NATIONS |
With an | ACCOMPANIMENT | for the | PIANO. |

1—VALLEY OF CHAMOUNI,	Glover	2½		2—JUANITA,	May	2½
3—WE'LL LAUGH AND SING,	Verdi	"		4—EVER OF THEE,	Hall	"
5—I KNOW A BANK,	Horn	"		6—THEY SAID MY LOVE WOULD CHANGE	Glover	"
7—ANNIE LAURIE,	Dunn	"		8—WHEN THE SWALLOWS,	Abt	"
9—THE SILVER MOON IS WATCHING,	Hallon	"		10—AH, I HAVE SIGH'D THEE TO REST,	Verdi	"
11—WHAT ARE THE WILD WAVES,	Glover	"		12—RUSTIC GATE,	Mori	"
13—KATHLEEN MAVOURNEEN,	Crouch	"		14—AGATHE,	Abt	"
15—DEAREST SPOT ON EARTH	Wrighton	"		16—WE MET BY CHANCE,	Kucken	"
17—MURMURING SEA,	Glover	3½		18—RATAPLAN,	Malibran	"
19—THE ANGELS,	Gumbert	2½		20—TEAR,	Gumbert	"
21—I'LL PRAY FOR THEE,	Donizetti	"		22—FAREWELL TO HOME,	Mengis	"
23—COME INTO THE GARDEN :	Balfe	4		24—HOME TO OUR MOUNTAINS,	Verdi	4
25—SADNESS MAKES THEE SWEETER;	Bellak	2½		26—SCENES THAT ARE BRIGHTEST,	Wallace	2½
27—DREAMS.	Hodges	3½		28—GOODNIGHT FAREWELL	Kucken	3
29—OH SUMMER NIGHT	Donizetti	2½		30—WHY DO SUMMER ROSES	Barker	2½
31—HAIL COLUMBIA,		2½		32—STAR SPANGLED BANNER,		2½
33—MARSEILLES HYMN,		"		34—'TIS NIGHT MY BARK IS ON THE OCEAN,	S. D. S.	3
35—WHERE ART THOU DEAREST,	Hall	"		36—AH, COULD I TEACH THE NIGHTINGALE,	Hall	2½
37—HER BRIGHT SMILE,		"		38—100 (empty)		
39—99 (empty)						

Published by JOHN CHURCH Jr. 66 West 4th St. |
CINCINNATI.

No date.

[165]

SONGS OF ALL NATIONS

With an ACCOMPANIMENT for the PIANO.

1	VALLEY OF CHAMOUNI.	Glover. 2½	2	JUANITA.	May 2½
3	WE'LL LAUGH AND SING.	Verdi. "	4	EVER OF THEE.	Hall "
5	I KNOW A BANK.	Horn. "	6	THEY SAID MY LOVE WOULD CHANGE	Glover. "
7	ANNIE LAURIE.	Dunn. "	8	WHEN THE SWALLOWS.	Abt "
9	THE SILVER MOON IS WATCHING.	Halton. "	10	AH, I HAVE SIGH'D THEE to REST.	Verdi "
11	WHAT ARE THE WILD WAVES.	Glover. "	12	RUSTIC GATE.	Mori. "
13	KATHLEEN MAVOURNEEN.	Crouch. "	14	AGATHE.	Abt. "
15	DEAREST SPOT on EARTH	Wrighton. "	16	WE MET BY CHANCE.	Kucken. "
17	MURMERING SEA.	Glover. 3½	18	RATAPLAN.	Malibran. "
19	THE ANGEL'S	Gumbert. 2½	20	TEAR.	Gumbert. "
21	I'LL PRAY FOR THEE.	Donizetti ..	22	FAREWELL TO HOME.	Menqis "
23	COME INTO THE GARDEN.	Balfe 4	24	HOME TO OUR MOUNTAINS.	Verdi 4
25	SADNESS MAKES THEE SWEETER.	Behak 2½	26	SCENES THAT ARE BRIGHTEST	Wallace 2½
27	DREAMS	Hodges 3½	28	GOODNIGHT FAREWELL	Kucken 3
29	OH SUMMER NIGHT	Donizetti 2½	30	WHY DO SUMMER ROSES	Barker 2½
31	HAIL COLUMBIA.	2½	32	STAR SPANGLED BANNER.	2½
33	MARSEILLES HYMN.	"	34	'TIS NIGHT MY BARK IS ON THE OCEAN.	S.B.S. 3
35	WHERE ART THOU DEAREST.	Hall. "	36	AH COULD I TEACH THE NIGHTINGALE.	2½
37	HER BRIGHT SMILE.	"	37		
39			40		
41			42		
43			44		
45			46		
47			48		
49			50		
51			52		
53			54		
55			56		
57			58		
59			60		
61			62		
63			64		
65			66		
67			68		
69			70		
71			72		
73			74		
75			76		
77			78		
79			80		
81			82		
83			84		
85			86		
87			88		
89			90		
91			92		
93			94		
95			96		
97			98		
99			100		

Published by JOHN CHURCH Jr. 66 West 4th St.
CINCINNATI.

STAR SPANGLED BANNER
Published by John Church Jr., Cincinnati.
Title-page. (Bib. No. 39.)

The title-page features a series of thirty-seven songs of which "STAR SPAN-GLED BANNER" is No. 32. The serial numbers from 38 to 100 are empty.

This edition is an exact copy of No. 30, the Dressler arrangement made in 1856 for the New York house of William Hall & Son. Dressler's name was omitted in Nos. 32, 36 and 36a, and is likewise omitted here.

Music and text fill pages 3-5. The caption title on page 3 reads: "THE STAR SPANGLED BANNER. | AMERICAN NATIONAL HYMN." The notation "Star Spangled Banner" appears in lower left hand corners of pages 4-5. Lower margin of page 5 bears the notation: "In the absence of a Choir, the Air may be sung as a Solo." Verso of page 5 is blank.

The date of this edition may be placed between 1859 and 1860. The publication of *Songs of all Nations* was John Church's earliest venture. Some of the pieces listed on the title-page appeared with his copyright notice and the dates of deposit 1859 and 1860.

There is a possible variation of the above. The writer has found an undated edition of "Home, Sweet Home," published by John Church Jr. 66 West 4th St. CINCINNATI, with a collective title-page. This pictorial cover, entitled: "The Home Circle, a collection of Standard Melodies," lists the "STAR SPANGLED BANNER" along with sixteen other songs. In the imprint, which is identical with the issue described above, the name of Beck & Lawton, Philadelphia, is one of several publishers' names added to that of John Church Jr. Beck & Lawton were actively engaged in the music publishing business in Philadelphia from 1857 to 1862. In 1863 the firm changed to J. W. Lawton. John Church, who entered the employ of Oliver Ditson of Boston in 1849, came to Cincinnati in April, 1859, and started in business for himself with Ditson as his senior partner. He was located at No. 66 West Fourth Street under the firm name of John Church Jr.

The approximate publication date of *The Home Circle* series of songs, therefore, would fall between 1859 and 1863, but whether the "STAR SPANGLED BANNER" ever appeared in this set cannot be verified, the writer never having seen a copy.

Between the years 1869 and 1872 John Church & Co. issued an uncopyrighted re-publication of the song with a new collective title-page of *Songs of all Nations,* which lists two columns of songs, seventy-two in all. No copy of "The Star Spangled Banner" with this new cover, however, has been located to date.

The names of Wm. A. Pond & Co., New York; C. W. A. Trumpler, Philadelphia; Lyon & Healy, Chicago are added to that of John Church & Co. in the publishers' imprint. In 1869 John Church Jr. bought out Ditson's share and changed the firm name to John Church & Co. In 1872 C. W. A. Trumpler was absorbed by F. A. North & Co. of Philadelphia. Thus the date of this reprint, if it actually appeared, must necessarily fall within the three year period above assigned.

Separate title page.

The | Star Spangled Banner | NATIONAL SONG. |
"O LONG MAY IT WAVE | OE'R THE LAND OF THE FREE | AND THE
HOME OF THE BRAVE." |
Stackpole, Sc. | SONG OR DUET | with CHORUS Ad Libitum. |

		Pr. 25 c. nett.
VARIATIONS 50	PIANO ARRANGEMENT	" 25 "
PIANO DUET 25	Do very easy	" 15 "

NEW YORK. | Published by WILLIAM DRESSLER, 933 Broadway. |
Also published "Close the Ranks Firmly." A famous song for the Union, sung with
great enthusiasm at the political meetings. Pr. 15 c. nett.

———————

No date.   Plate number 203-4 W. D.

The engraved title-page carries an almost full-page cut of the American flag with
thirty-four stars in its union, and the lines "O LONG MAY IT WAVE | OE'R THE
LAND OF THE FREE | AND THE HOME OF THE BRAVE." printed in the
middle of the field. Verso of title-page is blank. In some copies the title-page is printed
in color and in some in black and white or blue and white.

The same cover, omitting the notations: "VARIATIONS 50" and "PIANO
DUET 25" in the lower left hand corner, and "Do very easy 15," in the lower right,
served the publisher for the piano arrangement which was issued in 1861 with copyright notice, and, according to the files in the Library of Congress, was entered on
May 3, 1861. Whether this title cover was ever used for the uncopyrighted song
arrangement, however, is an open question. The writer has never seen a copy.

Music and text fill pages 3-5. The caption title on page 3 reads: "THE | STAR
SPANGLED BANNER. | NATIONAL SONG. | (Song or Duet with Chorus ad
libitum.) (Also just Published "CLOSE THE RANKS FIRMLY," a famous song
for the Union. Pr. 15 cts. nett.) | Arranged by WM. DRESSLER."

The music is an arrangement for voice and chorus for four voices with piano
accompaniment in 3/4 time in the key of B flat major. It is practically the same as
that of No. 30, except that the music is redivided from 6/4 time into 3/4 time and a
number of small note added in the melody. The bass part also has been changed, trans-
forming the piece into a waltz-like tune.

The text, which is the same as that of No. 30, is differently arranged. Verses
three and four, instead of appearing under the music on page 4, are interlined with
the music on pages 3 and 4.

The plate number appears in lower left hand corners of pages 3–5, and the
letters "W. D." are marked in the lower margins of the same pages. The lower right
hand corner of page 5 bears the name of the engraver "Pearson." Verso of page 5 is
blank.

This edition was published sometime during the year 1861.

[168]

THE STAR SPANGLED BANNER
Published by William Dressler, New York.
Title-page. (Bib. No. 40.)

WILLIAM DRESSLER
From a Photograph by Gessfort.
(By Courtesy of Mr. Joseph Fletcher, of Wm. A. Pond & Co., New York.)

This edition appeared with the same title-page in color, but the quotation: "O LONG MAY IT WAVE OE'R THE LAND OF THE FREE AND THE HOME OF THE BRAVE" omitted.

William Dressler, who had been musical editor of the New York firm of William Hall & Son since 1855, opened a music store of his own at No. 933 Broadway, with Charles O. Clayton, a noted New York music printer. Imprints of theirs appear in 1855 reading: "Dressler & Clayton, 933 Broadway." In 1861, Dressler removed to 927 Broadway, and again in 1866 to No. 926. During this period the firm went under the name of William Dressler.

No. 40b

When J. L. Peters, the Cincinnati publisher, transferred his business to New York in 1866, Dressler became the firm's adviser and proofreader. Peters re-published this edition of "The Star Spangled Banner" with his own imprint either during 1866, or within a year or so of this date.

1861   No. 41

Collective title-page.

National Music |

STAR SPANGLED BANNER, SONG

STAR SPANGLED BANNER, QUARTETTE

MARSEILLES HYMN, VOCAL |

MARSEILLES HYMN, INSTRUMENTAL |

HAIL COLUMBIA. |

J. H. BUFFORD'S LITH Boston |

YANKEE DOODLE. | 2½ [within star]

OUR FLAG IS THERE. |

BOSTON. Published by OLIVER DITSON & CO 277 Washington St. |

C. C. CLAPP & CO. Boston

BECK & LAWTON Philada.

FIRTH, POND & CO. N. York

JOHN CHURCH, JR. Cinn.

Entered according to Act of Congress in the year 1861 by Oliver Ditson & Co. in the Clerk's Office of the District Court of Mass.

BALLAD
Arranged for the
Piano Forte.
BOSTON.
Published by OLIVER DITSON & CO 277 Washington St.

**TITLE-PAGE OF "THOU HAST LEARNED TO LOVE ANOTHER,"
SHOWING VIEW OF OLIVER DITSON & CO.'S ESTABLISHMENT**
(By Courtesy of Mr. Malcolm N. Stone, West Englewood, N. J.)

Plate number 8612.

This is a copyright renewal edition and a reissue of the 1856 Ditson publication of the song. It was printed from the same plates, the original Atwill plates. The title-page, however, has been changed to the prevailing color-lithographed cover of the period, showing the American and French Republican flags crossed. The copyright notice appears in the lower margin of the title-page, verso of which is blank.

Music and text on pages 3-5 are the same as No. 29. Verso of page 5 is blank.

No. 41a

A variant of this title cover issued later, was also used for this publication. It is identical with the above one described except that the titles are differently arranged, and the song "AMERICA" is added to the list.

1861   No. 42

Separate title-page.

STAR SPANGLED BANNER. |
TRANSCRIBED FOR THE PIANO, | BY | Ch. Voss. |

[star]   [star]
2½ Song. | without Var; 3½   with Var: 5. |

G. ANDRÉ & Co, | 1104 Chestnut St. Philada.

Entered according to Act of Congress in the year 1861 by G. Andre & Co. in the Clerk's Office of the District Court of the Eastern District of Pennsylva.

_____

Copyrighted.   Plate mark G. A. & Co.

The decorative title-page is ornamented with a chromo-lithographed scene of a military camp, showing a Union soldier in the foreground holding a large American flag. The names "J. QUEEN DEL & LITH" and "P. S. DUVAL & SON LITH. PHILA." appear in the right and left corners respectively. The sides of this framed scene are flanked by war accoutrements connected with a fouled twin cable. The copyright notice is printed in the lower margin. Verso of title-page is blank.

This title-page was originally intended for a piano transcription of the "Star Spangled Banner" by Charles Voss, a popular German pianist and composer of many salon pieces.

The actual piano arrangement appeared in the following year with the old title-page retouched and elaborated. The figures in the camp-scene were slightly altered, the background became sub-tropical, and the whole was surrounded by an arched frame which supports an urn on either side. The rest of the cover is practically the same as in the previous copy. The publisher's copyright notice and date 1862 appear in the lower margin of the title-page. (See: No. 53.)

[173]

The last mentioned music cover was also used by G. André & Co. as early as 1861 for "Our Country's Flag," a civil war song dedicated to Abraham Lincoln.

S. T. Gordon of New York issued "The Star Spangled Banner Transcription by Charles Voss; Op: 242" in 1861, according to a signed and dated copy in the writer's collection. This publication which bears the (undated) copyright notice of N. Vanderbeck, N. Y., is entitled *"NATIONAL MELODIES,"* and lists, besides the above arrangement, other piano arrangements of "Star Spangled Banner," "Hail Columbia" and "Yankee Doodle" by different composers. The cover design, color-lithographed by Saroni, Major & Knapp, New York, shows the picture of a young boy in the act of nailing the national colors to a liberty pole.

Gordon used the same design in 1861 for "THE FLAG OF OUR UNION," a national song, with words by General Geo. P. Morris and music by William B. Bradbury. This publication bears the copyright notice of N. Vanderbeck, N. Y. and the year 1854 as date of entry.

The above music cover was probably copied from a very similar title design made in 1854 by A. Hoen & Co., the Baltimore lithographers, for H. McCaffrey, of Baltimore, and used by him for his "STAR SPANGLED FLAG OF THE FREE," a patriotic song, written by H. C. Preuss and composed by S. Macaulay.

Music and text of the Andre edition of the song fill pages 3–5. The caption title on page 3 reads: "THE STAR SPANGLED BANNER."

No arranger's name is given on the music, but it is the identical William Dressler arrangement originally made for and published by Wm. Hall & Son; New York in 1856 and attributed to Dressler. (See: No. 30.) This arrangement had not been copyrighted by Wm. Hall & Son, and, as has been mentioned, was subsequently pirated by a number of publishers.

The text is the same as in No. 28.

The firm's initials appear in lower margins of pages 3–5. Verso of page 5 is blank.

The piece was deposited for copyright on May 25, 1861. The writer, however, has a copy bearing the inscription "Miss Mary Dawson—May 23d 1861," and has seen one dated May 12, 1861, so it must have been in circulation shortly before that date.

The brothers Anton and Gustave Andre, descendants of the well-known André family of Offenbach, near Frankfort-on-the-Main, came to this country in the forties of the last century to engage in the music trade.

Anton, who stayed in New York, began business in 1843. He is listed in city directories until 1848 as Anthony André living and conducting his music store at No. 25 John Street. This address and firm name, however, does not check with that given copyrighted publications. Several of these pieces which have been examined bear the imprint: "André & Co. No. 447 Broadway, N. Y." and the copyright notice: "Entered. . 1848 by André & Co., New York." Possibly these publications are the work of Gustave André, who may have engaged in publishing in New York before he went to Philadelphia, or else perhaps the brothers were in business together for a short period. If there are any imprints bearing the name of A. André, they are very scarce. He is said to have printed little himself but to have imported foreign music largely classical. After 1848 he disappears from the records and is not found again until 1858, when Philadelphia city directories list him as a music teacher at No. 318 Cherry Street.

In 1850, Gustave, the more enterprising brother, opened a music shop at No. 19 South Fifth Street, Philadelphia. In addition to publishing a number of popular American numbers he imported and issued a considerable amount of European music, much of it published by his father's famous firm, Johann André of Offenbach. Three years later, in 1853, he formed the firm of G. André & Co. with Geo. E. Sourmann, Louis Olivier and Francis A. North as partners. They commenced business at No. 229 Chestnut Street, and in the following year removed their "Foreign Music Depot" to No. 19 South Ninth Street. Twice, between 1858 and the time for their dissolution, the firm moved to more spacious quarters, first at No. 1104 Chestnut Street and in 1872 or thereabouts at No. 1228, where, in 1879, the Oliver Ditson Company bought them out. Francis A. North, who withdrew from the Andre concern in 1870 and established his own business, was also absorbed by Oliver Ditson & Co. in 1890.

Brainard's Musical World, volume XII, (1875) reports the death of the André brothers: Gustave on December 18, and Anton on December 21, 1874.

1861   No. 43

Collective title-page.

HAIL COLUMBIA!!! | AND | STAR SPANGLED BANNER. |
WITH   ACCOMPANIMENT, | FOR THE | PIANO | BY |
SAMUEL JACKSON. |

NEW YORK. | PUBLISHED BY C. BREUSING, 701 BROADWAY.—
PRICE 25 c NETT. |

Entered according to Act of Congress in the year 1861, by C. Breusing in the Clerks office of the District Court of (of) the Southern District of N. Y.

———

STAR SPANGLED BANNER—The collective title cover displays a chromolithographed view of a Union officer carrying a large American flag, the Capitol in the background and soldiers marching towards it. On lower margin of the picture appears the notation: "Keating Delt." and "BOVELL, LITH N. YORK." The copyright notice is printed in lower margin of the title-page, verso of which is blank.

This same title-page was used for piano transcriptions of "The Star Spangled Banner" and "Hail Columbia," made by Geo. Wm. Warren and published by C. Breusing in 1861.

Music and text fill pages 3-5. The caption title on page 3 reads: "THE | STAR SPANGLED BANNER. | NATIONAL SONG | (WITH CHORUS AD LIBITUM.) Arranged by S. Jackson."

The music is an arrangement for voice and a chorus for four voices with piano accompaniment in 3/4 time in the key of B flat major.

[175]

WITH ACCOMPANIMENT,
FOR THE
PIANO
BY
Samuel Jackson.
NEW-YORK.
PUBLISHED BY C. BREUSING, 701 BROADWAY.   PRICE 25ᶜ NETT

STAR SPANGLED BANNER
Published by C. Breusing, New York.
Title-page. (Bib. No. 43.)

The text is the same as that adopted by Atwill in 1843. (See: No. 15.)

Samuel (P) Jackson, the arranger of this song and also of "Hail Columbia" had been an organist of note in several leading New York churches. He died in 1885 at the age of sixty. For many years Jackson was proof reader for Breusing and for Breusing's successor Gustav Schirmer.

This edition was deposited for copyright on June 8, 1861.

The New York publishing house of C. Breusing was founded in 1848 by Evich Kerksieg and Charles Breusing under the firm name of Kerksieg & Breusing. They commenced business at No. 421 Broadway. In or about 1854 Kerksieg withdrew and Breusing continued as sole owner at No. 701 Broadway until 1861. At that time B. Beer and Gustav Schirmer bought out the business. It was conducted for the next five years under the name of Beer & Schirmer, and in 1886 G. Schirmer obtained full control of it.

1861   No. 44

Collective title-page.

NATIONAL SONGS |
STAR SPANGLED BANNER   LA MARSEILLAISE |
YANKEE DOODLE   HAIL COLUMBIA. |
SUNG BY | MADLLE T. PARODI. |

NEW YORK | Published by S. T. GORDON, 706 Broadway. 2½ [within star]
Lith. of P. S. Duval & Son Phila.

Entd. according to Act of Congress, AD 1861, by S. T. Gordon in the Clerk's office of the Dt. Ct. of the Southern Dt. of N. Y.

The color-lithographed title-page displays the American and French Republican flags crossed. The American flag shows a constellation of thirteen stars. The design of this music cover is the same as of No. 32 and was copied from it. Verso of title page is blank.

Music and text fill pages 3–5. The caption title on page 3 reads: "The | STAR SPANGLED BANNER | An American National Hymn. | Duett Song & Chorus. | Arr. by S. T. Gordon." The copyright notice is printed in lower margin of page 3.

The music is an arrangement by S. T. Gordon for voice and chorus for four voices with piano accompaniment in 3/4 time in the key of B flat major.

The text is the same as that of the Atwill edition (No. 15).

The notation "Star" appears in the lower margins of pages 3 and 4, and the name "Porter" is found in the lower right hand corner of page 5. Verso of page 5 is blank.

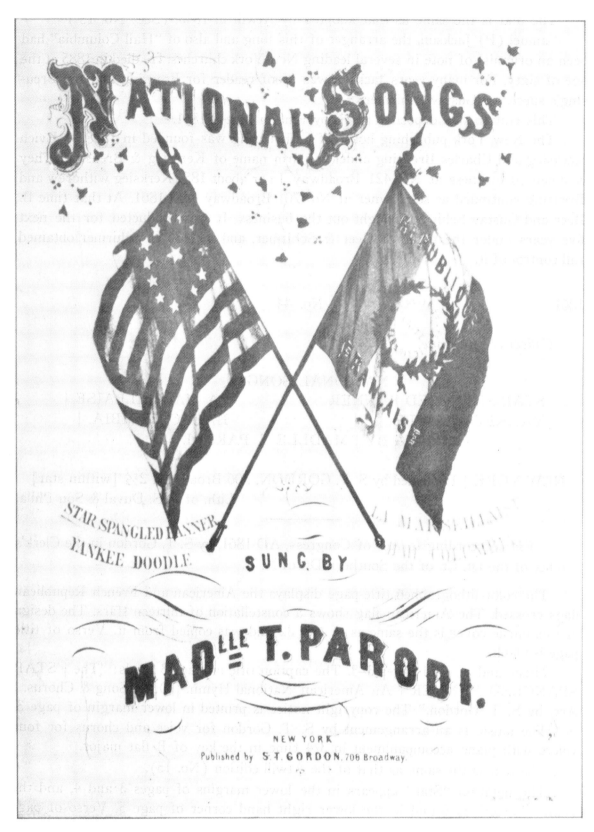

STAR SPANGLED BANNER
Published by S. T. Gordon, New York.
Title-page. (Bib. No. 44.)

STEPHEN THAYER GORDON
From a Photograph.
(By Courtesy of the Gordon Family.)

This edition appeared with a different title-page. It reads: "TO MISS RIACH. | 3 | AMERICAN | NATIONAL SONGS | WITH | Brilliant Variations | No. 1. STAR SPANGLED BANNER—No. 2 YANKEE DOODLE.—No. 3 HAIL COLUMBIA | Composed for the Piano, by | Henry Charles Becht. | (26th. Work) | P. M. Gaw. [engraver]—SONG 2½ [within star]—PIANO 5 [within star] | New YORK. | Published by S. T. GORDON. 706 Broadway."

Music and text on pages 3–5 are printed from the same plates as No. 44. Verso of page 5 is blank.

No. 44b

A reissue of No. 44 appeared with pages 3 and 4 printed from newly engraved plates and the original title-page and page 5 retained. Music and text of both issues, although somewhat different in the type-setting of the music and the lettering used in the caption title, are the same, except that the notation "Star" on the bottom of page 4 is omitted. The copyright notice is printed in lower margin of page 3.

No. 44c

Several variations of the same title-page were used for No. 44b. First it appeared with "AMERICA" "MY COUNTRY 'TIS OF THEE!" added to the songs listed on the title, and printed within the lower halves of the flag staffs.

(A copy of this variant is in the collection of Malcolm N. Stone, West Englewood, N. J.)

No. 44d

Later issues carried the notation: "SONG FOR THE UNION" printed in the upper halves of the flag staffs heading "AMERICA" "MY COUNTRY 'TIS OF THEE!" This variant, with "706" Broadway in the publisher's imprint changed to read "538" Broadway, was issued sometime during 1863 or after, the firm having removed to the latter address in the fall of 1863.

Stephen Thayer Gordon, the founder of the New York music publishing house of S. T. Gordon, was born in 1820 in Exeter, N. H., and there began his career as a church organist, teaching choirs and giving music lessons. Subsequently he studied in Boston under Lowell Mason. In 1846, at the advice of Mason and with the co-operation of Dudley Buck he went to Hartford, Conn., where he took the first steps in his eminently successful career as music publisher. About 1853–54 he came to New York and started in business with Oliver Ditson, J. E. Gould and T. S. Berry at No. 297 Broadway. The firm name, which up to this time (1855) had been Gould & Berry, was changed on January 1, 1854 to Berry & Gordon. In 1855 Gordon bought out Berry and subsequently Oliver Ditson and became the sole owner under the firm name of S. T. Gordon. In the course of time the firm absorbed many well known catalogues and grew to be one of the outstanding music publishing concerns in America. It afterwards moved to No. 736 and later to other addresses on Broadway. In 1861 the firm was located at No. 706 Broadway; S. T. Gordon died in 1890 at the age of seventy in Brooklyn, N. Y.

In 1870, Gordon's son Hamilton S. Gordon, became a partner and the firm, which was located at No. 13 East 14th Street, was known as S. T. Gordon & Son, until after the father's death, when it became Hamilton S. Gordon. Since the latter's death in 1914, the business has been conducted by the three grandsons of its founder, Leslie, Hamilton A., and Herbert Gordon. It is now located at No. 223 West 46th Street, New York.

1861   No. 45

Collective title-page.

OUR COUNTRY'S SONGS |

Star Spangled Banner.   Yankee Doodle. |
Hail Columbia.   Red, White & Blue. |
Stand by the Flag.   Vive l'America. |
Columbia rules the sea.   Unfurl the glorious Banner. |
Our Union right or wrong.   America. |

ALBANY J. H. HIDLEY.   CINCINNATI C. Y. FONDA |

NEW YORK. | PUBLISHED BY FIRTH, POND & CO. 547 BROADWAY |

Entered according to act of Congress in the year 1861 by Firth, Pond & Co. in the Clerks Office of the Dist. Crt of the So. Dist. of N. Y.

———

Copyrighted.   Plate number 1426.

The highly ornamental title-page is embellished with a color-lithographed oval, showing a young man holding a large American flag. A steam engine and a ship yard are seen in the background. The copyright notice appears under the picture. Verso of title-page is blank. (This cut was originally used by the publishers in 1855 for "THE YOUNG AMERICA SCHOTTISCH," composed by Francis H. Brown.)

Music and text fill pages 3–5. The caption title on page 3 reads: "THE | STAR SPANGLED BANNER! | Words by FRANCIS S. KEY.—Arranged by HENRY TUCKER."

The music is an arrangement for voice and piano with a chorus for four voices in 6/4 time in the key of B flat major.

The text was apparently copied from a Carr-type publication. It gives the mi placed word "was" in line 6 of the first stanza and the word "shall" in line 3 of the third verse.

The plate number is printed in lower left hand corners of pages 3–5, and the engraver's name "Clayton" is marked on lower margin of page 5, verso of which is

[181]

blank. Curiously enough, this number, 1426, is the same as the one used in the Firth, Pond & Co. edition described in No. 24.

45a

This edition was reprinted from the same plates with the same title-page by Wm. A. Pond & Co.

Late in 1862 John Firth relinquished his partnership in the old firm of Firth, Pond & Co. and early in 1863, opened his own store at No. 563 Broadway, doing business under the firm name of Firth, Son & Co. until 1866 when, as Thaddeus Firth, the concern ceased.

Meanwhile, in 1863, William A. Pond and John Maynal formed the firm of William A. Pond & Co. and continued in business at the old location. The new concern reissued a number of Firth, Pond & Co. publications, among them the set of *OUR COUNTRY'S SONGS*. These pieces, reprinted from the old plates with the imprint changed to read: "Wm. A. Pond & Co., 547 Broadway, N. Y.," appeared in 1864 and again in 1865.

(The New York firm of E. H. Harding, 229 Broadway, published this musical setting by Henry Tucker with a collective title-page in the early eighteen hundred and seventies. The text, however, is Atwill's version.) (No. 15.)

45b

A variant of No. 45 appeared with the numeral "2½ [within star]" printed in the lower half of the title-page.

1861   No. 46

Separate title-page.

THE | Star Spangled Banner | NATIONAL SONG |
"O LONG MAY IT WAVE | OE'R THE LAND OF THE FREE | AND THE
HOME OF THE BRAVE."
SONG OR DUET | with CHORUS | 2½ [within star]

NEW YORK | Published by HORACE WATERS 481 Broadway. |

Boston OLIVER DITSON & Co. 277 Washington St. |

Entered according to Act of Congress in the Year 1861 by E. A. Dagett in the Clerks Office of the District Court of the Southern District of New York.

Copyrighted.

The engraved title-page, with no engraver's name given, is similar to the one used by William Dressler in No. 40 and might have been designed by the same artist.
[182]

It shows a large American flag with thirty-three stars in its union and the notation: "O LONG MAY IT WAVE OE'R THE LAND OF THE FREE AND THE HOME OF THE BRAVE" in the middle of the field. Verso of title-page is blank.

Music and text appear on pages 2–4. The caption title on page 2 reads: "THE | STAR SPANGLED BANNER. | NATIONAL SONG. | (Song or Duet with chorus ad libitum.) Also Just Published, WHERE LIBERTY DWELLS, THERE IS MY COUNTRY. Price 25 Cts. | Arranged by AUGUSTUS CULL."

The music is an arrangement for voice and chorus for "Mixed Voices" and for "Male Voices" with piano accompaniment in 3/4 time in the key of A major.

The text contains the following variations from Key's original version: lines 2 and 3 of the first stanza read: "What so proudly we hail of the twilight's last gleaming; Whose broad stripes and the stars thro' the perilous fight" instead of: "What so proudly we hailed at the twilight's last gleaming; Whose broad stripes and bright stars thro' the perilous fight"; line 3 of the third verse reads: "A home and a country shall leave us no more" instead of "A home and a country should leave us no more," and line 6 of the same verse runs: "From the terror of flight o'er the gloom of the grave" instead of "From the terror of flight, or the gloom of the grave."

In the lower margin of page 4 appear the notations: "3rd Verse," "4th Verse" and "G. W. Ackerman Eng & Pr." Verso of page 4 bears an advertisement of "NEW MUSIC | JUST ISSUED BY | HORACE WATERS, No. 333 BROADWAY, NEW YORK." The address given here where the firm conducted business under the name of Horace Waters from 1852 until 1860, gives the misleading impression that the publisher had issued the song prior to 1861 without copyrighting it. Although certain music publishers, Lee & Walker of Philadelphia for example, (see: No. 36a), were not averse to using old announcements in this manner, this Horace Waters' issue was evidently taken in hand and engraved during the latter part of 1860 and copyrighted for circulation early in the following year when the firm was located at No. 447 Broadway. Subsequent publications of the song in book-form tend to prove this assertion. On May 21, 1861, the publisher copyrighted his *Day School Bell,* a collection of hymns and tunes, which contains Key's poem on page 145 with the old mistakes in the text corrected and line 3 of the first stanza changed to read "A home and a country 'should' leave us no more." The musical setting in the *Day School Bell,* however, is different from the one above. It is an arrangement in C major, by A. Cull, and appears on page 169 under the title "Freedom and Learning," a three stanza poem beginning: "When Freedom first came to America's shore . . etc." Later songbooks issued by Waters, among them the *Golden Harp, Choral Harp* and the *Athenaeum* copyrighted respectively April 14, May 16 and December 9, 1863, all carry the corrected version of the poem with the musical setting by Augustus Cull as first issued in sheet-song form.

No. 46a

A later issue of No. 46, brought out sometime during 1861 with a collective title-page, reads:

HORACE WATERS' |
Collection of | NATIONAL SONGS, |
Arranged for the | PIANO FORTE. |

No. 1. FLAG OF OUR UNION FOREVER.
" 3. STAR SPANGLED BANNER.
" 5 HAIL COLUMBIA.
" 7. WHERE LIBERTY DWELLS THERE IS MY COUNTRY.
" 9. VOLUNTEER YANKEE DOODLE OF 61.
" 11. THREE CHEERS FOR OUR BANNER.
" 13. HARK! THE SIGNAL.
" 15. WAR SONG OF THE N. Y. 69 REGT.

No. 2. OUR COUNTRY NOW & EVER. |
" 4. YANKEE DOODLE. |
" 6. FREEMEN'S GATHERING. |
" 8. { MY COUNTRY TIS OF THEE. | GOD SAVE OUR LAND. |
" 10. DRUMMER BOY OF THE NATIONAL GRAYS. |
" 12. MARCH ON! |
" 14. MADMEN SPARE THAT FLAG. |
2½ [within star]

NEW YORK | Published by HORACE WATERS, 481 Broadway. |
Boston O. DITSON & Co. 277 Washington St. |

Entered according to Act of Congress AD 1861 by E. A. Daggett, in the Clerk's Office of the District Court of the Southern District of New York |

IMP. BY CROW, THOMAS & Co, 37 PARK ROW, N. Y.

The ornamental title-page shows two American flags with a constellation of thirty-four stars in each union in color. The copyright notice appears in lower margin of title-page, verso of which is blank. Music and words of "No. 3 STAR SPANGLED BANNER" in this *Collection of National Songs*, fill pages 2–4 and are printed from the same plates as No. 46, with the faulty text. The copyright notice is repeated on page 2. Verso of page 4 is blank.

The same collective title-page was used with only eight of the fifteen songs listed. "WHERE LIBERTY DWELLS THERE IS MY COUNTRY," No. 7 of the pieces was advertised on the caption title of "No. 3 STAR SPANGLED BANNER," and actually appeared with this title cover, the writer having a copy of it in his collection. In all probability "The Star Spangled Banner" was also issued with this cover, although a copy of it is not on record.

Horace Waters (1812–1893, for many years the head of Horace Waters & Co., came to New York in 1845, opened a store at No. 447 Broadway and engaged in the sale of pianos. During the latter part of 1850 he combined with Thomas A. Berry, under the firm name of Waters & Berry. They removed to No. 333 Broadway in the following year and in 1851 dissolved partnership. Berry went in business with J. E. Gould, and Waters carried on alone at the same address where, in addition to selling musical instruments, he published sheet-music and music-books. In 1861 this flourishing business was removed to No. 481 Broadway, where it remained for over twenty years. Horace Waters gave up music publishing in May 1865, but continued as dealer in music and musical instruments for many years. His stock and catalogue was acquired by Charles M. Tremaine, who sold out to Charles W. Harris in 1869. S. T. Gordon eventually became the owner of it.

1861   No. 47

Collective title-page.

NATIONAL BEAUTIES |
STAR SPANGLED BANNER.   RED WHITE AND BLUE. |
YANKEE DOODLE.—2½ [within star]—HAIL COLUMBIA. |

As Performed by the, | UNITED STATES BRASS BAND. |

PHILADELPHIA. | Published by MARSH 1102 Chesnut St. |
Entered according to Act of Congress AD 1861 by Marsh in the Clerks Office of the Dist. Court of the Eastn. Dist of Pa.

———

Copyrighted.

The title-page of this édition of the "Star Spangled Banner" is ornamented with a pair of crossed flags in color; the American flag, showing thirteen stars, and the French the tricolor without the Republican insignia. The publisher's copyright notice appears in lower margin of title-page, verso of which is blank.

Music and text fill pages 3–5. The caption title on page 3 reads: "THE STAR SPANGLED BANNER. | AN AMERICAN NATIONAL HYMN. | Duett song and Chorus."

The music is an easy arrangement for voice and chorus for four voices with piano accompaniment in 3/4 time in the key of C major. No arranger's name is given.

The text is that of the Atwill (No. 15) edition.

Verso of page 5 is blank.

No. 47a

A variant of No. 47 shows the crossed flags on the title-page uncolored.

John Marsh, the publisher of this series of national songs, was noted during the years 1861 to 1865 for his patriotic songs, many of which he issued with highly colored and decorative title covers.

1861   No. 48

Collective title-page.

NATIONAL SONGS |

STAR SPANGLED BANNER.   LA MARSEILLAISE. |
YANKEE DOODLE.   HAIL COLUMBIA. |
            SUNG BY | MADLLE T. PARODI. |

2½ [within star]

RUSSELL & TOLMAN
New York   219 Washington Street.   Philadelphia.
S. T. GORDON.   BOSTON.   BECK & LAWTON.

Lith of P. S. Duval & Son Phila.

Ent'd. according to Act of Congress, AD 1861, by S. T. Gordon in the Clerk's office of the Dt. Ct. of the Southern Dt. of N. Y.

————

Copyrighted.

This edition is a republication of the Gordon edition (No. 44), printed from the same plates. The ornamental title-page is the same except for the change in the publisher's imprint.

Gordon's copyright entry appears in lower margin of page 3.

The address in the imprint, 219 Washington Street, however, is probably a misprint for 291 Washington Street. The firm of Russell & Tolman was located at the latter address from 1859 to 1861.

Henry Tolman, dealer in musical instruments and umbrellas, commenced business in 1855 at No. 153 Washington Street under the name of Henry Tolman. In 1856 and 1857 he was at No. 219 Washington Street, and in 1858 moved to No. 291. Here, in 1859 he went into partnership with George D. Russell under the firm name of Russell & Tolman. Russell left the firm during 1861 and Tolman, as Henry Tolman & Co., continued business at the No. 291 Washington Street address.

[186]

Collective title-page.

NATIONAL MUSIC |

VOCAL.	INSTRUMENTAL.
STAR SPANGLED BANNER.	STAR SPANGLED BANNER.	
MARSEILLES HYMN.	MARSEILLES HYMN.	
HAIL COLUMBIA.	HAIL COLUMBIA.	
YANKEE DOODLE.	YANKEE DOODLE.	
AMERICA.	AMERICA.	

OUR FLAG IS THERE. |

J. H. BUFFORDS LITH BOSTON—   2½ [within star]

BOSTON | Published by OLIVER DITSON & CO 277 Washington St. |

C. C. CLAPP & CO.	BECK & LAWTON
Boston	Philada.

FIRTH, POND & CO.	JOHN CHURCH JR.
N. York	Cinn

Entered according to Act of Congress in the year 1861 by Oliver Ditson & Co., in the Clerk's Office of the District Court of the District of Massachusetts.

Copyrighted.   Plate number 19950.

The title cover is ornamented with the American and French Republican flags in color. Verso of title-page is blank.

Music and text fill pages 3-5.

The caption title on page 3 reads: "THE STAR SPANGLED BANNER. | SONG & CHORUS. | With an additional verse (5th.) by DR. O. W. HOLMES."

The plate number appears in the right hand corners on lower margins of pages 3–5. Verse of page 5 is blank.

The music is an arrangement for voice and chorus for four voices with piano accompaniment in 3/4 time in the key of B flat major. No arranger's name is given.

Key's text is identical with Atwill's edition (No. 15) except that in line 3 of the first stanza, "Whose broad stripes and bright stars.. etc.," the word "broad" is omitted.

Holmes' additional stanza, the best-known of many such verses from time to time added to the poem, reads as follows: [17]

---

[17] Patriotic citizens often felt impelled to express themselves in heroic subjects by adding new verses to Key's poem. The earliest of these is the stanza suggested by the battle of New Orleans which was written by James Wilson of Wilmington, Del. and published in 1816 in *The Star-Spangled Banner*, "a collection of the best naval, martial and patriotic songs." The anthem is on page 14 and the extra stanza is printed with it:

STAR SPANGLED BANNER
Published by Oliver Ditson & Co., Boston.
Title-page. (Bib. No. 49.)

THE STAR SPANGLED BANNER.

SONG & CHORUS.

With an additional verse (5th) by Dr. O. W. HOLMES.

Con spirito.

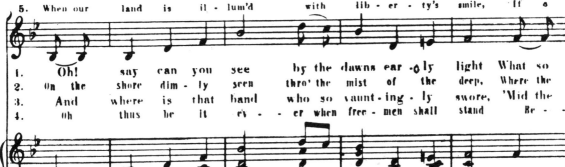

5. When our land is il-lum'd with lib-er-ty's smile, If a

1. Oh! say can you see by the dawns ear-ly light What so
2. On the shore dim-ly seen thro' the mist of the deep, Where the
3. And where is that band who so vaunt-ing-ly swore, 'Mid the
4. Oh thus be it ev - - er when free-men shall stand Be - -

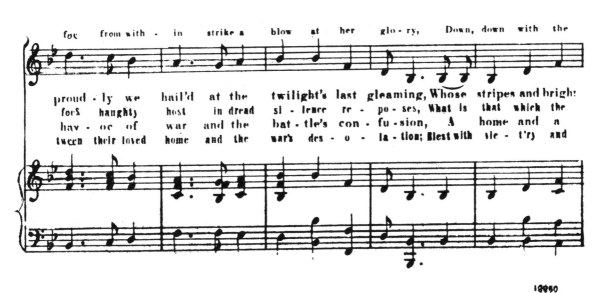

foe from with - in strike a blow at her glo-ry, Down, down with the

proud-ly we hail'd at the twilight's last gleaming, Whose stripes and bright
foes haughty host in dread si-lence re-po-ses, What is that which the
hav-oc of war and the bat-tle's con-fu-sion, A home and a
tween their loved home and the war's des-o-la-tion; Blest with vic-t'ry and

18960

STAR SPANGLED BANNER
Published by Oliver Ditson & Co., Boston.
Page [3]. *(Bib. No. 49.)*

STAR SPANGLED BANNER
Published by Oliver Ditson & Co., Boston.
Page [4]. *(Bib. No. 49.)*

STAR SPANGLED BANNER
Published by Oliver Ditson & Co., Boston.
Page [5]. (Bib. No. 49.)

"When our land is illum'd with liberty's smile,
If a foe from within strike a blow at her glory,
Down, down with the traitor that dares to defile
The flag of her stars and the page of her story,
By the millions unchain'd who our birthright have gained,
We will keep her bright blazon forever unstain'd!
And the star spangled banner in triumph shall wave
While the land of the free is the home of the brave!"

The "Publisher's Weekly" recently gave this stanza considerable publicity. The discussion in Mr. John T. Winterich's column, *Good Second Hand Condition* began on September 19, 1931 and lasted until November 19, 1932, producing a mass of valuable information.

Dr. Holmes, it seems, wrote two extra stanzas, which are to be found printed together for the first time in the 12-page pamphlet *Songs for the Fourth of July Celebration,* Boston, 1861. The earlier of these verses, apparently, first appeared in *Army Melodies; A Collection of Hymns and Tunes,* compiled by Rev. J. W. Dadmun, and published in Boston by Benjamin B. Russell, 515 Washington Street, undated but copyrighted April 15, 1861, and was also printed in *Songs of the Nation* for 1861, a songster published by Minard W. Wilson, New York, 1861, the copyright date of which is unascertainable. (Both these publications contain another "Star Spangled Banner" verse by Emma Stebbins, the New York sculptress. Her version, however, never appeared in music-sheet form.)

Holmes changed the form of his first additional stanza as follows: in the earlier version both lines 2 and 4 end with the word "glory," and line 5 reads "who our birthright have gained" for "when our birthright was gained."

This Ditson publication gives the latter version in line 4 and the earlier one in line 5. The date of copyright deposit is not on record.

This publication was included in *THE SILVER CHORD: A Collection of favorite Songs, Ballads, Duets, and Quartets,* issued in 1862 by the same publishers.

No. 49a

This edition appeared with the same title-page slightly changed. The list of songs is the same as in No. 49 except that the titles are printed closer together, and the headings "VOCAL" and "INSTRUMENTAL'" are printed in red instead of blue as above.

"Hail Jackson, Coffee and all the brave band
Who gallantly foiled the foes last demonstration . . . etc"

It was reprinted in *The Modern Songster,* Baltimore, 1825.

As recently as February 21, 1932, one of these new verses was written by Percy Mackaye for his masque *Wakefield* which was performed in Washington in celebration of the Washington Bicentennial.

Subsequent issues of No. 49 appeared with a newly color-lithographed title-page, which may be distinguished from the original one by its poorer workmanship. Otherwise it resembles the original with the following variations: the title, the imprint line and the copyright entry line are printed in different type and the lithographer's name is omitted; the numerals "2½" which appear within a star have in most cases been mutilated and changed into "3," and additional patriotic songs are listed in both vocal and instrumental form.

Probably the earliest variant of this title-page is the one which lists the same series of pieces printed in blue, and the headings in red, the same as in No. 44 and 44a.

No. 49c

This variant is furnished with a larger list of pieces printed in blue and the headings in red. "RALLY FOR THE BANNER" and "BEAR ON TO VICTORY" are added in the vocal series, and the instrumental section is changed to read: "STAR SPANGLED BANNER. OESTEN. | STAR SPANGLED BANNER. BEYER. | HAIL COLUMBIA. OESTEN. | HAIL COLUMBIA. BEYER. | YANKEE DOODLE. OESTEN. | YANKEE DOODLE. BEYER. | MARSEILLES HYMN. BEYER. | AMERICA. BEYER." The numeral "3" within a star, instead of being printed in the right hand corner of the page, the same as in all the aforementioned numbers, appears in the upper part, between the vocal and instrumental sections.

1861 No. 50

Collective title-page.

NATIONAL MELODIES |

1. STAR SPANGLED BANNER.
2. HAIL COLUMBIA.
3. LA MARSEILLAISE.
4. YANKEE DOODLE.
5. GOD SAVE THE QUEEN.
6. RULE COLUMBIA.
7. SWORD OF BUNKER HILL. (SONG) (QUARTETTE)
8. OUR COUNTRY'S STARRY FLAG. |

3½ [within star]

L. PRANG & CO. LITH. BOSTON

CLAPP & CORY.
PROVIDENCE.

ROOT & CADY.
CHICAGO.

BOSTON | PUBLISHED BY RUSSELL & TOLMAN 291 WASHINGTON ST. |

Entered according to act of Congress AD 1861 by Russell & Tolman in the Clerks Office of the District Court of Mass.

[193]

STAR SPANGLED BANNER
Published by Russell & Tolman, Boston.
Title-page. (Bib. No. 50.)

THE STAR SPANGLED BANNER.

SONG OR DUETT AND CHORUS.

Originally written by Francis S. Keys with an additional verse (5th) by Dr. O. W. Holmes.

Arr. by C. BRUEN.

1. O say can you see by the dawn's early light, What so proudly we hail'd at the
2. On the shore dimly seen thro' the mists of the deep, Where the foe's haughty host in dread

twilight's last gleaming; Whose broad stripes and bright stars thro' the perilous fight, O'er the ramparts we
silence reposes, What is that which the breeze, o'er the towering steep, As it fitfully

watch'd were so gallantly streaming, And the Rocket's red glare, the bombs bursting in air, Gave
blows, half conceals, half discloses; Now it catches the gleam of the morning first beam, In full

Entered according to act of Congress AD 1861 by Russell & Tolman in the Clerk's Office of the District Court of Mass.

STAR SPANGLED BANNER
Published by Russell & Tolman, Boston.
Page [3]. (Bib. No. 50.)

STAR SPANGLED BANNER
Published by Russell & Tolman, Boston.
Page [4]. (Bib. No. 50.)

free   and the   home   of the brave.

free   and the   home   of the brave.

free   and the   home   of the brave.

free   is the   home   of the brave.

3.

And where is that band, who so vauntingly swore,
'Mid the havoc of war and the battles confusion,
A home and a country they'd leave us no more, —
Their blood has washed out their foul footsteps' pollution.
No refuge can save the hireling and slave,
From the terror of flight or the gloom of the grave;
And the star spangled banner in triumph doth wave,
O'er the land of the free and the home of the brave.

4.

O thus be it ever, when freemen shall stand
Between their loved homes and the war's desolation;
Blest with victory and peace, may the heaven rescued land
Praise the power that has made and preserved us a nation.
Then conquer we must, when our cause it is just,
And this be our motto — "In God is our trust" —
And the star spangled banner in triumph shall wave,
O'er the land of the free and the home of the brave.

5.

When our land is illumined with Liberty's smile
If a foe from within strike a blow at her glory,
Down, down with the traitor that dares to defile
The flag of her stars and the page of her story!
By the millions unchained, when our birthright was gained
We will keep her bright blazon for ever unstained —
And the star spangled banner in triumph shall wave,
While the land of the free is the home of the brave.

3365

STAR SPANGLED BANNER
Published by Russell & Tolman, Boston.
Page [5]. (Bib. No. 50.)

The highly colored and decorative title cover displays four flags crossed; the American, French Republican, British and Italian. Verso of title-page is blank.

Music and text fill pages 3–5. The caption title on page 3 reads: "THE STAR SPANGLED BANNER. | SONG OR DUETT AND CHORUS. | Originally written by Francis S. Keys with an additional verse (5th,) by Dr. O. W. Holmes. | Arr. by C. Bruen." The author's name is misspelled "Keys." The copyright notice appears in lower margin of page 3.

The music is an arrangement by C. Bruen for two voices and a chorus for four voices with piano accompaniment in 3/4 time in the key of B flat major.

The text is the same as that of Atwill's edition (No. 15).

The plate number appears in the lower margins of pages 3–5. Verso of page 5 is blank.

The extra verse by O. W. Holmes, which is printed on page 5 under the Key poem, is the later version of the poem, giving the word "story" in line 4, and with line 5 reading "when our birthright was gained."

Since the copyright deposit date of this edition is unavailable, it is impossible to ascertain whether the ever alert Oliver Ditson, (No. 49) or the smaller Boston firm of Russell & Tolman was first to issue Holmes' additional stanza in sheet-music form. Perhaps some of Dr. Holmes' biographers can tell the story.

(This same version (with the Holmes extra stanza) was issued in 1875 in sheet form by White, Smith & Co. of Boston. It appeared together with Key's text and the music of "The Star-Spangled Banner; As originally written" (by T. Carr). The same publishers printed it in the May, 1875, number of their publication *Folio: A Journal of Music, Drama, Art and Literature,* Boston, 1869–1895.)

No. 50a

NATIONAL MELODIES.

1861

Collective title-page.

Vocal.		
No.		[star]
1.	STAR SPANGLED BANNER,	2½
2.	HAIL COLUMBIA,	2½
3.	YANKEE DOODLE,	2½
4.	ROCK OF LIBERTY,	Quartette.. 3
5.	SWORD OF BUNKER HILL,	Song.. 3
6.	SWORD OF BUNKER HILL,	Quartette.. 3
7.	OUR COUNTRY'S STARRY FLAG,	3
8.	GRAND UNION MEDLEY,	5
9.	MARSEILLAISE,	2½
10.	GOD SAVE THE QUEEN,	2½
11.	STAND BY THE UNION,	3

Instrumental.		
No.		
12.	STAR SPANGLED BANNER,	Baumbach, 4
13.	STAR SPANGLED BANNER, (Simplified,)	do. 2½
14.	YANKEE DOODLE & HAIL COLUMBIA,	do. 2½
15.	MARSEILLAISE,	do. 2½
16.	COLUMBIA, THE GEM OF THE OCEAN,	do. 2½
17.	YANKEE DOODLE, (Variations,)	White, 3
18.	GRAND UNION POTPOURRI,	Baumbach, 5
19.	GRAND UNION POTPOURRI, (4 hands,)	do. 5
20.	HAIL COLUMBIA,	De Meyer, 6
21.	YANKEE DOODLE,	do. 6
22.	GOD SAVE THE QUEEN,	Czerny, 3

BOSTON: |

Published by Russell & Tolman, 291 Washington St.

S. T. GORDON,
NEW YORK.

CLAPP & COREY,
PROVIDENCE.

ROOT & CADY,
CHICAGO.

Entered according to act of Congress AD 1861 by Russell & Tolman in the Clerks Office of the District Court of Mass.

Plate number 3363.

[199]

STAR SPANGLED BANNER
Published by Russell & Tolman, Boston.
Title-page. (Bib. No. 50a.)
(By Courtesy of Mr. A. B. Hunt, Brooklyn, N. Y.)

Except for a new lithographed title-page, this edition is a reissue of No. 50 and printed from the same plates. The title-page displays a large American flag in color with a constellation of thirty-four stars, and lists twenty-two numbers in both vocal and instrumental form.

No. 50b

A reissue of the above edition, printed from the same plates appeared with the same title-page changed to read: "BOSTON: Published by Henry Tolman & Co. 291 Washington St.," and the firm name "Henry Tolman & Co." substituted in the copyright notice line for that of "Russell & Tolman."

Both publications, according to their copyright notice, were issued in 1861. At the close of this year Russell & Tolman dissolved partnership. G. D. Russell withdrew and later on formed the firm of G. D. Russell & Co. at No. 126 Tremont Street. Tolman, under the firm name of Henry Tolman & Co. continued in business for a number of years at No. 291 Washington Street. In 1869 he removed to No. 289 Washington Street and in 1870 he is recorded at No. 27 Worcester Square.

A renewal edition was issued in 1889.

A copy of it is in the Library of Congress.

HENRY TOLMAN
Drawn from a Photograph by Max Jacobs.

TITLE-PAGE OF "EXCELSIOR POLKA," SHOWING VIEW OF
RUSSELL & TOLMAN'S ESTABLISHMENT, BOSTON

Collective title-page.

NATIONAL MELODIES |
STAR SPANGLED BANNER   THE STRIPES AND THE STARS |
HAIL COLUMBIA   GOD SAVE OUR COUNTRY'S FLAG |
LA MARSEILLAISE   MY COUNTRY 'TIS OF THEE |

2½ [within star]

EHRGOTT, FORBRIGER & Co. LITH. CINCINNATI. |

CLEVELAND | Published by S. BRAINARD & CO. 203 Superior St.

_____

No date.   Plate number 345.3.

The collective cover of this series of patriotic songs is ornately color-lithographed with small standards embedded in the title on top of the page and with the American and French flags in the centre.

Music and text of "Star Spangled Banner" fill pages 3–5. The caption title on page 3 reads: "THE STAR SPANGLED BANNER | AMERICAN NATIONAL HYMN."

The music is a setting for voice and a chorus for four voices with piano accompaniment in 3/4 time in the key of B flat major. It is a blend of No. 30 and No. 40, and, although no arranger's name is given, it is apparently another arrangement made by William Dressler. The present version is practically the same as in No. 30 except for a few rhythmic changes in the melody, the omission of the grace notes, as in No. 40 and the simplification in several places of the piano part.

The text is the same as that used in No. 30 and in all subsequent Dressler arrangements.

The plate number appears in lower margins of pages 3-5. The lower right hand corner of page 5 bears the name: "J. J. Lemon. Engr:" Verso of page 5 is blank.

No. 51a

The same title-page as above appeared with two more numbers, "BATTLE PRAYER" and "BANNER SONG," added to the series of six songs listed. The price mark was changed to "3" on this variant.

No. 51b

Another variant appeared with the numeral "3" changed to "3½."

The present song, which heads this series of *National Melodies* was not copyrighted, but all the other pieces, which have come to the compiler's attention, were deposited for copyright and bear the publishers' notice: "Entered..AD 1861 by S.

STAR SPANGLED BANNER
HAIL COLUMBIA
LA MARSEILLAISE

THE STRIPES AND THE STARS
GOD SAVE OUR COUNTRY'S FLAG
MY COUNTRY 'TIS OF THEE

CLEVELAND
Published by S. BRAINARD & Cᵒ 203 Superior St.

STAR SPANGLED BANNER
Published by S. Brainard & Co., Cleveland.
Title-page. (Bib. No. 51.)

STAR SPANGLED BANNER
Published by S. Brainard & Co., Cleveland.
Page [3]. (Bib. No. 51.)

3

And where is that band, who so vauntingly swore
That the havoc of war and the battle's confusion
A home and a country shall leave us no more,
Their blood has washed out their foul footsteps pollution
No refuge could save the hireling and slave,
From the terror of flight or the gloom of the grave
And the star spangled banner, in triumph shall wave,
O'er the land of the free, and the home of the brave.

4

O! thus be it ever when freemen shall stand,
Between their lov'd home and the war's desolation,
Blest with victory and peace, may the heaven rescued land
Praise the Pow'r that has made and preserv'd us a nation.
Then conquer we must, when our cause it is just,
And this be our motto, In God is our trust;
And the star spangled banner in triumph shall wave,
O'er the land of the free, and the home of the brave.

R.W. 30.

STAR SPANGLED BANNER
Published by S. Brainard & Co., Cleveland.
Page [4]. (Bib. No. 51.)

STAR SPANGLED BANNER
Published by S. Brainard & Co., Cleveland.
Page [5]. *(Bib. No. 51.)*

Brainard & Co. . . " in the lower margin of page 3. It is, therefore, safe to presume that "The Star Spangled Banner" either was published prior to 1861 or appeared early in that year when patriotic airs were in great demand.

Of particular interest in this bibliography is one of the songs in this set of National Melodies, "THE STRIPES AND THE STARS," A "NEW VERSION OF THE MELODY OF THE STAR SPANGLED BANNER. SONG OR DUET AND CHORUS. Words by Edna Dean Proctor. Adapted and arranged by Wm. Dressler." The issue bears the publishers' notice of copyright entry and date 1861. The music is practically the same as Dressler's arrangement of No. 40 except that a number of small notes have been changed in order to fit the melody to the Proctor poem. Copyright records give November 26, 1861, as date of deposit.

Silas Brainard (1814–1871), who founded the Cleveland music publishing firm of the same name in 1836 and in 1845 commenced to issue his own publications, was noted for the variety of his musical publications and for his patriotic pieces during the Civil war period. After Brainard's death, his two sons Charles S. and Henry M. Brainard continued in business for many years under the firm name of Brainard's Sons & Co. They also opened a branch in Chicago.

[1861]   No. 52

Separate title-page.

Star Spangled Banner |

NATIONAL SONG | Pearson N. Y. (eng.)
NEW YORK | Published by JOHN J. DALY 419 Grand St.

No date.

The engraved title-page is ornamented with a pair of crossed American flags in color, with each union showing twenty-five stars. Verso of title-page is blank.

Music and text fill pages 3–5. The caption title on page 3 reads: "STAR SPAN-GLED BANNER."

The music is an arrangement for voice and a chorus for four voices with piano accompaniment in 3/4 time in the key of B flat major. No arranger's name is given.

In the text line 3 in the third stanza reads: "A home and a country should leave us no more." The first line of the same verse reads: "And where is that band which so vauntingly swore" instead of "And where is that band who so vauntingly swore," and in the first line of the fourth stanza which should read: "And the Star Spangled Banner in triumph 'shall' wave," the word 'doth' was used.

The word "Pearson" appears in the lower right hand corner of page 5, verso of which is blank.

This edition, which has been assigned the year 1861 as the time of its appearance, carries neither plate number or any other tell-tale mark whereby this date may be verified. Like the majority of "Star Spangled Banner" issues described in this bibliography it is not mentioned in the *Complete Catalogue of Music and Musical Works published by the Board of Trade, New York, 1870.*

It could have been published prior to 1861; John J. Daly, who started in the music trade in 1849 at No. 233½ Walker Street, New York, is recorded at No. 419½ Grand Street from 1852 to 1869, except in 1860 and 1865, when directories list him at No. 419 Grand Street. His imprint, though, invariably reads: "419 Grand St."

The writer, however, assumes 1861 to be approximately correct, having found this piece along with a number of patriotic songs in a bound volume of sheet music all of which were copyrighted in 1861. The book itself bears the former owner's name and date "1861," embossed on the outside cover.

1862   No. 53

Separate title-page.

50TH. EDITION. |
STAR SPANGLED BANNER. |
TRANSCRIBED FOR THE PIANO, | BY | Ch. Voss. | G ANDRÉ & Co. | 1104 CHESTNUT ST. PHILADA. | [star] | without Var. 3½ [within shield] | with Var. 5 [within shield] |

Entered according to Act of Congress in the year 1862 by G. André & Co., in the Clerk's Office of the District Court of the Eastern District of Penna.

———————

Copyrighted.

The ornamental color-lithographed title-page is the same as the one described in No. 42 which was used for the piano arrangement by Charles Voss and for "Our Country's Flag." (See: No. 42.) The copyright notice appears in the lower margin of the title-page, verso of which is blank.

Music and text fill pages 3–5. The caption title on page 3 reads: "THE | STAR SPANGLED BANNER."

The complete piano arrangement of the air appears on page 3 and the voice part with piano accompaniment on pages 4 and 5. The music is an easy arrangement in 3/4 time in the key of C major. No arranger's name is given.

The text is almost the same as in No. 8. The word "was" is misplaced in line 6 of the first stanza and the word "broad" omitted in line 3 of the same verse. A new error appears in line 3 of the first stanza, ("Whose stripes and bright stars"): the word "stripes" is misspelled "stipes."

Verso of page 5 is blank.

STAR SPANGLED BANNER
Published by G. André & Co., Philadelphia.
Title-page. (Bib. No. 53.)

THE
STAR SPANGLED BANNER

STAR SPANGLED BANNER
Published by G. André & Co., Philadelphia.
Page [3]. (Bib. No. 53.)

STAR SPANGLED BANNER
Published by G. André & Co., Philadelphia.
Page [4]. *(Bib. No. 53.)*

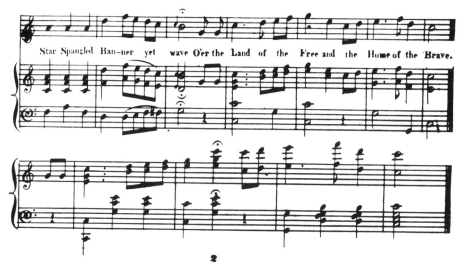

Star Spangled Ban-ner yet wave O'er the Land of the Free and the Home of the Brave.

2

On the shore dimly seen thro' the mists of the deep,
   Where the foe's haughty host in dread silence reposes;
What is that which the breeze, o'er the towering steep
   As it fitfully blows, half conceals, half discloses;
Now it catches the gleam of the morning's first beam,
In full glory reflected, now shines in the stream—
'Tis the Star Spangled Banner, Oh! long may it wave,
O'er the Land of the Free, and the Home of the brave.

3

And where is that band who so vauntingly swore,
   That the havoc of war and the battle's confusion,
A home and a country shall leave us no more—
   Their blood has wash'd out their footstep's polution
No refuge could save the hireling and slave
From the terror of flight, or the gloom of the grave;
And the Star Spangled Banner in triumph doth wave,
O'er the Land of the Free and the Home of the brave

4

Oh thus be it ever when Freemen shall stand
   Between their lov'd home, and the wars desolation;
Blest with vict'ry and peace, may the Heaven rescu'd land,
   Praise the Pow'r that hath made and preserved us a nation:
And this be our motto—"In God is Our Trust"
And conquer we must, when our cause it is just,
And the Star Spangled Banner in triumph shall wave,
O'er the Land of the Free and the Home of the brave.

STAR SPANGLED BANNER
Published by G. André & Co., Philadelphia.
Page [5]. *(Bib. No. 53.)*

[1864-1866]
Collective title-page.

No. 54

GATHERED PEARLS
A COLLECTION OF | BEAUTIFUL SONGS
BY
VARIOUS AUTHORS.

JUANITA OR WANETA.	Mrs. Norton	2½	KATHLEEN MAVOURNEEN	Crouch	3
THEN YOU'LL REMEMBER ME.	Bohemian Girl	"	HOME, SWEET HOME	Bishop	2½
HEAR ME NORMA (Duett)	Norma	3½	OFFICERS FUNERAL.	Mrs. Norton	"
WHAT ARE THE WILD WAVES. (Duett)	Glover	2½	HER BRIGHT SMILE.	Wrighton	"
AH! I HAVE SIGHED TO REST ME.	Trovatore	"	DO THEY THINK OF ME AT HOME	Glover	"
WE MET BY CHANCE	Kucken	"	COMIN' THRO' THE RYE	Scotch	"
STAR SPANGLED BANNER		"	ASK ME NOT WHY	Child of the Regiment	"
Geo. F. Swain.					

Philadelphia
Published by W. R. SMITH Agt. 135 N. Eight St.

———

No date.

[215]

Verso of engraved title-page is blank.

This edition of which music and text fill pages 3–5 is identical with the edition published by G. André & Co. Philadelphia, in 1862 (No. 53) and is printed from the same plates.

It was issued between the years 1864 and 1866. William R. Smith, the Philadelphia music dealer, makes his first appearance in city directories in 1861 as a merchant at No. 1324 North Eleventh Street. In 1863 he is listed as a music dealer at No. 933 Spring Garden, (residence: 1324 N. 11 St.). From 1864 to 1866 records list him as "agent music & musical instruments" at No. 135 North Eighth Street, (residence 1324 N. 11 St.) In the following year his address is No. 825 North Eighth Street.

ADDENDA

While this book was in proof sheets, the writer's attention has been called to a sheet-song publication which seems to bear out his contention that the Osbourn plates of "Yankee Doodle," "Hail Columbia," and "Star Spangled Banner," (see No. 12,) were acquired and issued by Ld. Meignen & Co., who subsequently sold them to J. C. Smith. (See No. 17.)

It is a separate publication of "Hail Columbia," printed on two unpaged inside pages from the Osbourn plates with the publisher's imprint changed to read: "Philadelphia. Ld. MEIGNEN & Co. 217 Chesnut St." and the plate number "625" substituted for that of Osbourn. However, whether Smith, who used Ld. Meignen & Co.'s plate numbers "620" and "623" respectively, for his reprint of "Yankee Doodle" and "Star Spangled Banner," also issued "Hail Columbia" cannot be ascertained until a copy of it comes to light.

LIST OF MATERIAL IN LIBRARIES, HISTORICAL

INSTITUTIONS AND PRIVATE COLLECTIONS USED AND DESCRIBED

IN THIS BIBLIOGRAPHY.

(The writer would welcome any additional information.)

KEY.

AAS	American Antiquarian Society, Worcester, Mass.
ABH	Arthur Billings Hunt, Brooklyn, N. Y.
BPL	Boston Public Library.
BUL	Brown University Library, Providence, R. I.
FLP	Free Library, Philadelphia.
GL	Grosvenor Library, Buffalo, N. Y.
HCL	Harvard College Library, Cambridge, Mass.
JFD	J. Francis Driscoll, Brookline, Mass.
LC	Library of Congress.
M	Joseph Muller, Closter, N. J.
MHS	Maryland Historical Society, Baltimore, Md.
NYPL	New York Public Library.

Numbers:

AAS	2a, 7, 24, 24a, 35
ABH	8, 15, 24, 33, 37b, 44c, 45, 50a
BPL	3, 20, 29, 49
BUL	5, 22, 30, 37, 41, 45
FLP	6a, 36a
GL	22, 28, 29, 33, 37, 37a, 42, 44, 46, 48, 53
HCL	2, 3, 7, 8a, 10, 15, 16, 19, 27, 29, 30a, 36, 42, 44, 44b, 45, 45a, 46, 49, 49a, 50b
JFD	5, 6a, 7, 8a, 9, 15, 16, 19, 27, 29, 33, 33a, 35, 36, 38, 43, 45, 46, 47, 49, 50, 50b
LC	1, 1a, 2, 3, 3a, 4, 5, 6, 6a, 6b, 7, 8a, 9, 11, 12, 13, 14, 15, 16, 16a, 17, 18, 19, 22a, 23, 24, 25a, 26, 26a, 27, 27a, 28,28a, 29, 30a, 31, 31c, 33a, 34, 35, 36, 36a, 37, 37a, 37b, 37c, 39, 40, 40a, 40b, 42, 43, 44, 44a, 44b, 44d, 45, 45b, 46, 47, 49, 49a, 49b, 49c, 51, 51a, 52, 53
M	2, 4, 5, 6a, 7, 8a, 13, 15, 27, 33a, 34, 39, 43, 44, 45, 51
MHS	1
NYPL	1, 3, 10, 13, 20, 22, 24, 37b, 46

INDEX

Ackerman, G. W., 109, 183
"Adams and Liberty," 20, 20n, 34
Adams, John, 20n
"A Life on the Ocean Wave," 88
"America," 173, 180
American Antiquarian Society, 20n
"The American Flag," 162
American National Songs, 134, 146, 151
"Anacreon in Heaven" *See* "To Anacreon in Heaven,"
"The Anacreontic Song" 15n, 20n
André, Anton, 174
André, Gustave, 174, 175
André, G., & Co., 173, 174, 175, 210
"And since you leave me," 71
Army Melodies: A Collection of Hymns and Tunes, 192
Ashton, John, 103
Ashton, John, & Co., 103
Ashton, John, Jr., 103
"A Song for American Freedom," 11
Atwill, Joseph F., 87, 91, 96, 100, 109, 111, 173

Bacon, Allyn, 64
Bacon, A., & Co., 28, 61, 64, 70, 90
Bacon & Hart, 64, 71
Bacon, Weygand & Co., 64
Baltimore American, 25n
Baltimore Patriot, 25n
"The Banjo", 124
Barnum, P. T., 35
"The Battle of the Wabash", 52
Beacham, J. R., 100
Beacham, Joseph R., 123
Beam, W. Ward, 27
Beanes, Dr. William, 23
Becht, Henry Charles, 180
Beck & Lawton, 167
Beer, B., 177
Beer & Schirmer, 177
"Before the Lord We Bow", 23
Benteen, F. D., 99, 123
Benteen, Frederick D., 80, 90, 100
Benteen, F. D., Jr., 100
Berry, T. S., 180
Berry & Gordon, 180
"Beauties of Beethoven", 146
Bickerstaff's Boston Almanac, 1769, 11
Bieber, A. A., 162
"The Birthday of Freedom", 35
Bishop, Henry R., 80
Bishop, T. Brigham, 153
Blackmar, A. E., 29

Blake, George F., 52
Blodgett, J. R., 159
Blodgett & Bradford, 159, 161, 162
Boswell, James E., 101, 102
Bovell, 175
Bradbury, William B., 174
Bradford, 161
Bradlee, Charles, 86, 103
Bradlee, C., & Co., 86
Brainard, Charles S., 209
Brainard, Henry M., 209
Brainard's Musical World, 175
Brainard, Silas, 209
Brainard Sons & Co., 209
Brainard, S., & Co., 29, 204, 209
Breusing, Charles, 175, 177
Broadsides, Nicholson-Waters, 25n
Broadsides, Müller, Niklas, 25n
Broadsides, Price, Julia, 25n
Broadsides, Sweet, F. G., 25n
"Broadway Sights", 99
Brooks-Aten, Mrs. Florence, 36
Brown, Francis H., 87, 91, 96, 99, 109, 126, 181
Bruen, C., 198
Buds and Blossoms, 157
Buck, Dudley, 180
Bufford, J. H., 126, 140
Butts, General, 29n
"Buy a Broom", 80

"The California Pioneers", 99
Callender, Joseph, 12
"Call freedom triumphant", 39n
Campbell and Hoogs San Francisco and Sacramento City directory, 96
Carr, B., & Co., 39n
Carr, Benjamin, 39, 39n
Carr family, 12
Carr, Joseph, 39, 41, 49
Carr, Mary Jordan (Merryman), 42, 44
Carr, Milcah (Merryman), 41
Carr, Thomas, 27, 28, 39–46, 57, 67, 73, 80, 119, 129, 198
The Carrs, 39
The Carrs, American Music Publishers, 28
Carrs Music Store, 27
"Castles in the Air", 153
Centennial Exposition, 119
"Charley's Quick Step", 104
Chase, George W., 104
Choral Harp, 183
Church, John, 167
Church, John, Jr., 167

Church, John & Co., 167
Clayton, Charles O., 171, 181
"Close the ranks firmly", 168
Cochrane, Admiral, 23
Cole & Hewes, 75
Cole, George F., 80
Cole, John, 42, 75, 80, 86, 90, 99, 100, 123
Cole, John & Son, 80
Cole, Samuel, 75
Collection of National Songs, 184
*Columbia a Collection of American National
    Melodies,* 113, 118
"Come down to the Latice," 75
"Comin' Thro' the Rye", 88
Coo, Jacques, 99
Cooper, Samuel A., 87
"Count Benyowski", 52
"Cross of the South", 29
Crown and Anchor Tavern, 13, 49
Cull, Augustus, 183
Custis, Eleanor Parke, 20n

Dadmun, Rev. J. W., 192
D'Almaine & Co., 119
Daly, John J., 209
Darley, F. O. C., 99
Davenport, L. E., 84
Day School Bell, 183
"Death of General Wolfe," 12
Deems, James M., 100
"Defence of Fort M'(Mc)Henry," 25, 27, 57
Dickinson, John, 11
Dickson, James A., 88
Dielman, Louis H., 41
Ditson, J. E., & Co., 119
Ditson, Oliver, 103, 104, 111, 126, 167, 180
Ditson, Oliver, & Co., 86, 104, 112, 117, 119, 123,
    146, 153, 154, 155, 171, 175, 187
Dressler & Clayton, 171
Dressler, William, 129, 145, 167, 168, 171, 174,
    182, 209
Dubois, William, 111
Dubois & Warriner, 111
Dubois & Stodart, 111
Duval, P. S., 140
Duval, P. S., & Son, 173

"Early Secular American Music," 12
Eckerson, Mrs. Charles, 96
Eckhard, Jacob, Senior, 34
"El Eco Del Pacifico," 99
Ellerbrook, James, 29
Emerson, L. O., 122n
Engelbrecht, J. C., 100
"E Pluribus Unum," 36
Ethiopian Serenaders, 122

Fillmore Executive Mansion, 102

Fiot, A., 90, 91
Fiot, August, 91
Fiot, Meignen & Co., 91, 101
Firth & Hall, 28, 80, 84, 86, 112
Firth, Hall & Co., 84
Firth, John, 84, 112, 162, 182
Firth & Pond, 84
Firth, Pond & Co., 31, 112, 162, 181, 182
Firth, Thaddeus, 182
Fischer, William, 146
Fischer, William Arms, 86
'The Flag of our Union," 174
Flowers of the South, 153
The Folio, 198
"For the glorious Fourteenth of July," 15
"Fort Mc.Henry, or, The Star Spangled Ban-
    ner," 56, 57
Foster, Shephen C., 100
"Freedom and Learning," 183
"Freedom and Peace," 34
"Freedom triumphant," 39n

Gathered Pearls, 215
Gaw, P. M., 180
Geib, Adam, 64, 67
Geib, 'A. & W., &'Co., 67
Geib & Co., 64
Geib & Jackson, 67
Geib, George, 67
Geib, George H., 67
Geib, John, Senior, 64
Geib, John, Junior, 64
Geib, John and Adam, & Co., 67
Geib, J. A. & W., 35, 67
Geib, John, & Co., 64
Geib & Walker, 35, 67
Geib, William H., 67
"Geneva," 75
Gilfert, G., 20n
Gillingham, 164
Golden Harp, 183
Golden Wreath, 122n
"Good night and pleasant dreams," 124
Good Second Hand Condition, 192
Gordon, Hamilton A., 181
Gordon, Hamilton S., 181
Gordon, Herbert, 181
Gordon, Leslie, 181
Gordon, Stephen T., 174, 177, 180, 185, 186
Gordon, S. T., & Son, 180
Gottschalk, L. M., 124
Gould, John E., 91, 180, 185
Gould & Berry, 180
Goulding & D'Almaine, 80
Granger, C. H., 104
Graupner, Gottlieb, 12, 103
Gregory, James G., 99
Grobe, Charles, 146, 157, 159

Hagen, P. A. von, & Co., 20n
"Hail Columbia," 175
Hall & Sellers, 11
Hall, James F., 112
Hall, William, 84, 112
Hall, William, & Son, 28, 84, 86, 99, 111, 112, 124, 129, 145, 155, 167, 171, 174
Harding, E. H., 182
Hardinge, 52, 57
Harris, Charles W., 185
Harrison, William Henry, 42, 52
Hart, Abraham L., 64
Hawthorne, Alice, 159
Hayes, John C., 104
"Hearts of Oak," 11
Hewitt & Jaques, 87, 88, 89
Hewitt, James, 20n, 35, 39, 89
Hewitt, James L., & Co., 88, 89
Hewitt, James Long, 88
Hewitt, John Hill, 88
"The Highlander March," 140
Higgins, H. M., 29
Higgins Brothers, 29, 153
Hill, Thomas Clifford, 28
"The Hill Tops," 12
"History of the American Pianoforte," 84
Hoen, A., & Co., 174
Holland, Edwin C., 34
Holmes, Oliver Wendell, 31, 187, 192, 198
Home Lighting Co., 41
"Home, Sweet Home," 23
Homer, Winslow, 126
Hoover, President, 36
Howard, John Tasker, 88
Howe, William, 20n
Hull, Asa B., 31
Hupfeld, Charles, 91

"I greet thee gentle flower," 145
"I'll love Thee in the Spring Time," 99
"In the lonely grove I linger," 104
"I see them on their winding way," 88

Jackson, Samuel (P), 175, 177
Jaques, Edward I., 87, 89
Jarvis, Charles, 89
"Jim Crow," 140
Jollie, Samuel C., 96, 109, 111, 126

Keating, 75
"The Kentucky Volunteer," 13
Kerksieg & Breusing, 177
Kerksieg, Evich, 177
Key, Francis Scott, 15, 23–25, 46, 96
Key, John Ross, 23
Key, Philip Barton, 23
Klemm, A. F., 70
Klemm & Brother, 70, 71

Klemm, Johann Gottlob, 70
Klemm, John G., 70, 71
Knowles collection, 28, 39, 41
Knowles, Mahlon Bunting, 28
"Kossuth Grand Reception March," 146
Krantz, G. Fred., Music Company, 164

Latham, W. H., 99
Lawton, J. W., 162, 167
Lee & Walker, 145, 146, 151, 157, 159, 183
Lee, Julius, 146
Lemon, J. J., 204
Lewis & Brown, 96
Lincoln, Abraham, 174
Lind, Jenny, 145
Linley & Moore, 20n
Loder, E. J., 119, 122
Longman & Broderip, 15, 15n
"Lord, With Glowing Heart I Praise Thee," 23
"Lorena," 31
Love, Miss, 80
"Love Not Quick Step," 100
Lyon & Healy, 167
"Lyra Sacra," 23

Macaulay, S., 174
MacKaye, Percy, 192n
Magazine
    The American, 12
    The Analectic, 27
    The Boston, 12
    The Century Illustrated Monthly, 46
    The Columbian, 12
    The Massachusetts, 12
    The New York, 12
    The Pennsylvania, 12
    The Royal American, 12
    The Vocal, or British Songster's Miscellany, 13
Maretzek, M., 145
Marsh, John, 185, 186
Mason, Lowell, 180
Masonic Harp, 104
Maxwell, Wm., 58
Maynal, John, 182
McCaffrey, H., 29, 174
McHenry, Dr., 27n
Meignen Ld., & Co., 91, 101
Meignen, Leopold, 91
Mein & Fleming, 11
Meineke, C., 75
Merkley, C., 119, 134
Merryman, Milcah, 41
Mesier, E. S., 80
"Militia Military Association of Philadelphia," 34
Miller & Beacham, 100, 123
Miller, Frederick W., 89
Miller & Osbourn, 23, 89
Miller, William C., 100, 123

Millet, William E., 84, 102
Mills, J. M., 162
Minden, 23
Morris, Geo. P., 174
Musical America, 27
Musical Bouquet, 122
The Musical Quarterly, 28
Music for the Union, 136
Music Publishers in New York City before 1850, 87

National Beauties, 185
National Hymns, 35
National Jubilee, 27n
National Melodies, 193, 199
National Music, 171, 187
National Songs, 124, 140, 157, 177, 186
National Songs of America, 126, 129
Naval Songs; Wm. A. Pond & Co., N. Y. 1905, 61
Neal, Wills & Cole, 58, 61, 80
"Nellie Dear Lies Sleeping," 153
New Grotto Concert Saloon, 25n
"New Star-Spangled Banner," 29
Nicholson, Judge, 25
North, Francis A., 167

Oldman, C. B., 122
"Old Tippecanoe Raisin," 42
Olivier, Louis, 175
Osbourn, James G., 89, 100, 101
Our American Music, 88
"Our Country's Flag," 174, 210
Our Country's Songs, 181, 182

Paine, Robert Treat, 20
Parker, Samuel H., 104
Parodi, Teresa, 140, 145, 157, 177, 186
Paul, Mrs., Howard, 122
Pearson, J. C., 129, 159, 161, 168, 209
Pearson & Melville, 124
Pease, Alfred H., 162
Pendleton, Cooper Hunt, 46
Peters, A. C., & Bro., 139, 140
Peters, Cragg & Co., 139
Peters, Field & Co., 139
Peters, J. L., & Bro., 112, 139, 140
Peters, John L., 119, 134, 140, 171
Peters, W. C., & Sons, 34, 139
Peters, William Cumming, 139
Peticolas, L. C., 29
"Philadelphia Quadrilles," 89
Philips, T., 35
Pierpont, Rev. John, 36
"The Pillar of Glory," 34
Pond, Sylvanus B., 84, 86
Pond, William A., 84, 182
Pond, Wm. A., & Co., 162, 167, 182

Porter, 177
The Port Folio, 34
Prang, L., & Co., 193
Preuss, H. C., 174
Price, Julia, 25n
Proctor, Edna Dean, 29, 209
"Publisher's Weekly," 192

Queen, J., 173
Quirot & Co., 99

Redway, Mrs., Virginia Larkin, 28
Reinagle, Alexander, 12
Rice, T. D., 140
Richard & Mallory, 58
Richter, Dr. M. A., 99
Riley, E., 35
"Rise Columbia, Brave and True," 34
Rosenthal, L. N., 140
Russell, Benjamin B., 192
Russell, George D., 186, 201
Russell, G. D., & Co., 201
Russell & Tolman, 186, 193, 198, 199, 201

Sarony & Major, 145
Sarony, Major & Knapp, 174
Schetky, George, 12
Schirmer, Gustav, 177
Shaw, Joseph P., 161, 162
Shaw, Oliver, 42n
Shaw, Robert, 12
Sheard, C., 122
The Silver Chord, 192
Sinclair, T. S., 140, 146
Skinner, John S., 23
Smith, J. C., 100
Smith, Jonathan C., 101
Smith, John Stafford, 15
Smith, William R., 215, 216
Smithers, J., 12
"Song for the Union," 180
Songs of all Nations, 167
Songs of the Nation, 192
Songsters
  American Muse, New York, 1814, 27
  American patriotic and comic modern songs, Newburyport, 1814, 27n
  The American Star, second edition, Richmond, 1817, 27n
  The Columbian Songster, New York, 1797, 15
  The Modern Songster, Baltimore, 1825, 192n
  The National Songster, Hagers-Town, 1814, 27
  The New American Songster, Philadelphia, 1817, 27n
  The Star Spangled Banner, Wilmington, 1816, 27n, 187n
Sonneck, O. G. (T.), 12, 15, 52, 57, 58, 84
Sourmann, Geo. F., 175

"The Southern Cross," 29
Sparrow, 103
Spilane, D., 84
"The Star Spangled Banner"
    Additional stanzas, 188n, 192
    Broadsides, early, 25n
    Carr-type editions, 28, 49, 58, 61, 64, 70, 71, 75, 86, 87, 89, 90, 99, 100, 101, 102, 103, 111
    Composer—See "To Anacreon in Heaven"
    Hewitt version, 35
    History of text, 23–27
    First printed, 27, 49
    First published in music-sheet form, 27, 28, 49
    First publisher, 27, 28, 49
    Parodies, etc., 27n, 29, 30, 42n, 52, 183, 192
The Star Spangled Banner, O. G. T. Sonneck, 1914, 15
"The Star-Spangled Banner: Yesterday and To-day," 27
"Star Spangled Flag of the Free," 174
Stebbins, Emma, 192
Stone, Ellen, 31
Stone, Malcolm N., 134, 180
Strakosh, Maurice. 143
"The Stripes and the Stars," 209
Strunk, Oliver, 27
"Sweet By and By," 31
Sweet, F. G., 25n
Sweetser, Mrs. J. Emerson, 99

Taney, R. B., 23
Taw, Joseph, 42
Taylor, C. W., 88
Taylor, Raynor, 12. 13, 20, 34
Temperance Annual and Cold Water Magazine for 1843, 29
The Temperance Rallying Songs, 31
"The Appeal of the Reformed Inebriate," 31
"The Birthday of Freedom," 35
"The Castilian Maid," 71
"The Golden Stair," 31
"The Home of the Soul," 23
"The Lavender Girl," 88
"The Liberty Song," 11
"The Minstrels return from the war," 88
"The Pillar of Glory," 34
"The Whigs of Columbia shall surely prevail," 42n
"The young May Moon," 41n
"This Blooming Rose at Early Dawn," 35
Thomas & Andrews, 20, 20n
"To Anacreon in Heaven"
    American history, 15
    Author, 13
    Composer, 15
    Origin, 13
    Parodies, etc., 20, 35, 42, 52
    Popularity in America, 36
Tolman, Henry, 186

Tolman, Henry, & Co., 201
Tomlins, James, 58
Tomlinson, Ralph, 13, 49
Tremaine, Charles M., 185
Tripp & Cragg, 139
Trumpler, C. W. A., 167
Tucker, Henry, 181
Tucker, St. George, 29
"Turn Out! To the Rescue!" 42

Vanderbeck, N., 174
Vestris, Madame, 80
The Vocalist, 155
Vogt, George, 145
Voss, Charles, 173, 174, 210

Wade, E. H., 103
Walker, William, 146
Wakefield, 192n
Wallace, W. V., 124
Walters, Henry, 25n
Warren, George Wm., 175
Warrington, James, 42
Washington, General, 12
Washington Bicentennial, 192n
Washington National Intelligencer, 27, 58
Waters & Berry, 185
Waters, Horace, 182, 183, 185
Waters, Horace, & Co., 185
Webster, Joseph P., 29, 31
Weikert, Constantine, 145
"Welcome Fayette," 42
Werlein, P. P., & Co., 29
"When all thy mercies, o my God," 75
"When Death's gloomy Angel was bending his bow," 20
"Where Liberty dwells there is my Country," 185
White, Edward L., 104
White, Richard Grant, 35
White, Smith & Co., 198
White, Smith & Perry, 198
White, William, 122
"Williams Light Infantry Quick Step," 87
Willig, George (Philadelphia), 12, 20, 28n, 71, 78, 146
Willig, George, Junior, 42, 71, 73, 87, 90, 164
Willig, George, & Co., 164
Willig, Henry, 164
Willig, Joseph E., 164
Willson, Charles. 162
Willson, John M., 161, 162
Wilson, A., 34
Wilson, James, 87n
Wilson, Minard W., 192
Winner & Shuster, 157, 159
Winner, Septimus. 159
Winterich, John T., 192
Wittig, Rudolph, 140, 145, 157

"Ye Seamen of Columbia," 58
"The Young America Schottisch," 181

SUPPLEMENT

UNRECORDED EARLY PRINTINGS OF
THE STAR SPANGLED BANNER

By Lester S. Levy and James J. Fuld

❖

In the thirty-five years that have passed since Joseph Muller's excellent bibliography of *The Star Spangled Banner*,[1] a number of additional early printings of our national anthem have been found, and it seems desirable to record them while they are fresh in mind.

In determining which additional printings to describe, the authors have used Muller's test, namely, "Words and Music issued between 1814–1864." Not deemed of sufficient interest to report, however, are mere variants of editions already described by Muller. Muller's general manner of presentation has been continued.

That early editions of *The Star Spangled Banner* are not lacking in interest is shown by the price of $23,000 paid at an auction by a dealer for one of the nine known copies of the first edition of *The Star Spangled Banner*.[2] This is believed to be the highest price ever paid for a piece of printed music.

Before his descriptions of the early editions of *The Star Spangled Banner*, Muller mentions certain other interesting printings that relate to the anthem, and here, also, a number of additional printings have recently been discovered. Thus, following Muller's description of the first edition of *The Star Spangled Banner* by Carr of Baltimore, he describes on page 52 *The Battle of the Wabash* published by G. E. Blake, Philadelphia, with the words of *The Star Spangled Banner* added. He was not aware that about 1828 J. Siegling, 109 Meeting Street, Charleston, S. C., also published *The Battle of the Wabash*, with the words of *Fort McHenry or the Star Spangled Banner* following the music and text at

Mr. Levy, Pikesville, Md., author of *Grace Notes in American History* (Norman: University of Oklahoma Press, 1967), has lectured frequently on aspects of American popular music. His second book, *Flashes of Merriment* (University of Oklahoma Press), is to appear in the spring of 1971. Mr. Levy's well-known private library of American popular sheet music has been used extensively by scholars in many fields.

Mr. Fuld, New York, author of *The Book of World-Famous Music* (New York: Crown Publishers, 1966) and *A Pictorial Bibliography of the First Editions of Stephen C. Foster* (Philadelphia: Musical Americana, 1957), is a lifelong bibliographer and collector of first editions of well-known classical, popular, and folk music of all countries from 1600 to date.—Ed.

[1] New York, G. A. Baker & Co., 1935.
[2] Part Two of the Thomas W. Streeter Collection, Parke-Bernet Galleries, New York, 20 April 1967, item number 1068.

the bottom of the second page. A copy of this edition is in the Lilly Rare Book Library of the University of Indiana. Furthermore, Muller reported on page 35 an arrangement of the words of *The Star Spangled Banner* with an original melody by James Hewitt of New York, who also published the song in 1819. Subsequent publications by others utilizing the Hewitt air were mentioned by Muller on the same page. Since the issuance of Muller's bibliography, another edition of *The Star Spangled Banner* with Hewitt's melody, published about 1855 by J. E. Gould, Philadelphia, has come to light. A copy is in the collection of Lester S. Levy, Pikesville, Maryland. Still another edition of *The Star Spangled Banner,* with Hewitt's melody, published by D. P. Faulds, Louisville, about 1855, is known to have existed, but we are presently unable to locate a copy.

About 1816, G. Willig's Music Store, Philadelphia, published *Washington Guards*, written by John F. Wells of the Third Company of the Washington Guards, to the air of *Anacreon in Heaven*. On the verso of the second page appear the words of the four verses of *Fort McHenry or The Star Spangled Banner as Sung by Mr. Hardinge*. Copies of this edition are in the Library of Congress, the New York Public Library, and the private libraries of Lester S. Levy and Mrs. Josephine L. Hughes (Charleston, S. C.).

To Muller's descriptions of fifty-four early editions of *The Star Spangled Banner,* we are adding below fifteen additional early printings.

No. 55   [1842]

YANKEE DOODLE / & / STAR SPANGLED BANNER / *Philadelphia,* LD. MEIGNEN & CO., *217 Chesnut St.*

Collective title page. No date. Plate numbers 620, 625, 623.

This edition is an issue of a collection of three songs. YANKEE DOODLE is printed on the outside page (1), and HAIL COLUMBIA on the two inside pages (2) and (3). The caption title on page (2) reads: The popular National Air, / HAIL COLUMBIA / WITH / YANKEE DOODLE & STAR SPANGLED BANNER / Composed & Simplified / FOR THE / PIANO FORTE. The publisher's imprint is the same as on page (1). Copy at Lester S. Levy.

The caption title on page (4) reads STAR SPANGLED BANNER.

Yankee Doodle, plate number 620; Hail Columbia, plate number 625; Star Spangled Banner, plate number 623.

This edition is a reprint of the edition of Osborn's Music Saloon, 30 S. 4th St., Philadelphia (see Muller No. 12).

No. 56   [1844–59]

THE / Star Spangled Banner. / N York Published by LEWIS H. EMBREE, 134 Bowery

No separate title page. No date. No plate number.

The title is ornamented. This Carr-type edition has music and text which fill two unpaged inside pages. The second page also includes an arrangement for the flute. Copies at Lester S. Levy and James J. Fuld.

Lewis H. Embree was a bookseller, stationer, and clerk from 1844 to 1872. He was at 134 Bowery from 1844 to 1859.

No. 57 [1845–1848]

The STAR SPANGLED BANNER / Arranged for the / Spanish Guitar / Philadelphia LEE & WALKER 120 Walnut St / New Orleans W. T. MAYO No. 5 Camp St

No separate title page. No date. Plate number 570–2.

The title is ornamented, and there is a burst of stars. Music, in C major in 6/4 arranged for the Spanish guitar, and text fill two unpaged inside pages. Neither the name of the author nor of the arranger is given. Copy at James J. Fuld.

The firm of Lee & Walker is traced in Muller, p. 146, where the years 1845–48 are given for the address at 120 Walnut St. W. T. Mayo was also probably at the address indicated above during these years.

No. 58 [1846–1855]

THE STAR SPANGLED BANNER / NATIONAL SONG / Written during the / BOMBARDMENT OF FORT MC HENRY / BALTIMORE, BY THE LATE / FRANCIS S. KEY ESQ^R, / St. Louis BALMER & WEBER 56 Fourth St.

No separate title page. No date. Plate number 617–2.

Music and text fill the two inside pages in this Carr-type publication. The arrangement is in 3/4 and in C major, exactly like

Muller No. 7 (John Cole, Baltimore). As in this earlier edition, the word "broad" is omitted from line 3 in the first stanza, and the word "was" is misplaced in line 6. Copy at Lester S. Levy.

No. 59 [1852]

The / STAR-SPANGLED BANNER, / National Song / *Arranged for* / FOUR VOICES / Written during / THE / Bombardment of Fort McHenry / *Baltimore, by the late* / FRANCIS S. KEY ESQ^R, / *Gillingham eng. 25 cts. net* / *Published by* F. D. BENTEEN & Co. *Baltimore* / *Wm. T. Mayo New Orleans*

Separate title page. No date. Plate number 2349.

Music on pp. 2–5. Verso of page 5 blank. Copies at Library of Congress and Lester S. Levy.

Music is in 3/4 time, in C major, and is

scored for four voices with piano accompaniment.

Caption at the top of p. 2 reads: THE STAR-SPANGLED BANNER/FOR FOUR VOICES. In right-hand lower corner of p. 5 appears the name "Webb."

No. 60 [1855–1858]

NATIONAL / SONG / STAR SPANGLED BANNER / HAIL COLUMBIA / YANKEE DOODLE / MARSEILLES HYMN / 2½ [within star] / *L. Gery, Eng.* / PUBLISHED / BY / P.P. WERLEIN, 5 CAMP ST. NEW ORLEANS / PATTEN & BLACKMAR / VICKSBURG / G. HERRDMAN / BATON ROUGE / FIRTH POND & CO. / NEW YORK

Collective title page. No date. Plate number 175.

The title page is ornamented with crossed flags and ornate shield. Verso of title page blank.

Music and text on pp. 3–5. The caption title on p. 3 reads: THE STAR SPANGLED BANNER / AMERICAN NATIONAL SONGS / No. 5 / Arranged by WM. BRESSLER. Copy at Lester S. Levy.

The music is an arrangement for voice with piano accompaniment in 6/4 time in

the key of B-flat major. The plates are those used by William Hall & Son, 239 Broadway, New York (see Muller No. 30), except that Hall's plate number was eliminated and Werlein's substituted.

Philip P. Werlein took over the W. T. Mayo business at 5 and 7 Camp St. in 1854 and remained in business in New Orleans under his own name until 1879, except for three years during the period of the Civil War when his business was shut down.

No. 61 [1855–1862]

Home Melodies / A SELECTION OF FAVORITE / SONGS AND BALLADS / BY / VARIOUS AUTHORS /

No. 1 THE PARLOR FIRE Freligh 2½
" 2 I WANT TO GO HOME Orpheus 2
" 3 I WOULD LIKE TO CHANGE MY NAME 2½
" 4 ADELLA MAINE 2½
" 5 COME BE QUEEN OF THE FOREST 2½
" 6 INDIANS LAMENT FOR HIS TRIBE 3
SONG OF THE WILD HORSE 3
CASTLES IN THE AIR 3
HER BRIGHT SMILE HAUNTS ME STILL 3

No. 7 THE BELLES MISTAKE Freligh 3
" 8 THE BROKEN CHAIN Woolcott 2½
" 9 ROSALIND Oriscus 2½
" 10 I STOOD ON THE SHORE 3
" 11 MARY'S AWAY 3
" 12 WILD-WOOD BIRDS 3½
" 13 SAINT'S ETERNAL HOME Mrs. Harris 3
STAR SPANGLED BANNER 2

Published by BALMER & WEBER 56 Fourth Street, / St. LOUIS / NEW YORK / Firth, Pond & Co. / BUFFALO / Sheppard & Cottier

Separate title page. No date. Plate number 617-2.
The five lines of collective title are extremely ornamented. Page 2 states "NATIONAL SONG / Written during the / BOMBARDMENT OF FORT McHENRY / BALTIMORE, BY THE LATE / FRANCIS S, [*sic*] KEY ESQr," followed by the publisher's imprint. Music, in C major in 3/4, and text fill pp. 2-3. Copies at Lester S. Levy and James J. Fuld.
In 1846 Charles Balmer and Henry Weber took over the Shepard & Phillips business and continued music publishing until 1907. The publication dates of 1855-62 are derived from the imprints of the co-publishers.

No. 62 [1860]

NATIONAL SONGS / STAR SPANGLED BANNER / YANKEE DOODLE / LA MARSEILLAISE / HAIL COLUMBIA

SUNG BY / MADLLE T. PARODI. / Philadelphia by BECK & LAWTON 7th & Chestnut St. / Successors to J. E. GOULD / Boston OLIVER DITSON & CO. T. CARTWRIGHT, Wheeling Va. TRUAX & BALDWIN Cincinnati / New York S.T. GORDON / Lith of P.S. Duval & Son Phila.

Collective title page. No date. No plate number.
This edition displays the same colored music cover and the same music and text as Muller No. 32. Music and text are on pp. 3-5. Verso of p. 5 is blank. Copy at Lester S. Levy.

No. 63 [1860]

THE / HOME CIRCLE / A collection of / Standard Melodies /

HOME SWEET HOME	2	MY SISTER DEAR	1½
ANGELS WHISPER	2½	MY MOTHER DEAR	1½
FAIRY BELLS	2	IT IS BETTER TO LAUGH	2½
HAIL COLUMBIA	2	SWITZER'S FAREWELL	2½
STAR SPANGLED BANNER	1½	COMING THR'O THE RYE	1½
I DREAMPT THAT I DWELT	2½	THEN YOU'LL REMEMBER ME	
IN HAPPY MOMENTS	1½		1½

MY HOME MY HAPPY HOME	2½	HEART BOW'D DOWN	1½
MARY OF ARGYLE	1½	FAREWELL MY FATHERLAND	2½

CINCINNATI / Published by John Church Jr. 66 West Fourth St. / Oliver Ditson & Co., / *Boston* / Beck & Lawton / *Philada.* / Firth Pond & Co. / *N. York* / *Eng. by Greene & Walker, Boston*

Collective title page. No date. Plate number 17.

The title page is ornamented at the top with a group of people playing pianoforte and singing.

Words and music on pp. 2-3. Verso of p. 3 blank. Copy at Lester S. Levy.

Pages 2 and 3 are from the plates of Muller No. 2 (the A. Bacon & Co., Philadelphia, edition) but with Bacon's name and address omitted and no other name replacing it. Plate number is that of Muller No. 2A.

No. 64   [1860–1862]

THE STAR SPANGLED BANNER

Re-arranged and brought within an easy compass for Chorus Singing, by Wm. B. BRADBURY 427 Broome St., New York

No separate title page. No date. No plate number.

This is a four-part vocal arrangement in 3/4 in A major. The single page, embellished with ornamental border, has words of the first verse indicated with the music. Words of third and fourth verses are printed beneath the musical arrangement. Copy at Lester S. Levy.

William B. Bradbury commenced the publishing of music in 1855 at 427 Broome Street and 122 Wooster St., New York. He discontinued publishing at Wooster Street in 1860 but continued at various Broome Street addresses until 1867.

No. 65   [1861–1862]

Patriotic songs / of the / United States of America / newly arranged for voice and / PIANO-FORTE / and published by J. Schuberth & Co. New York /

No. 1. The Star spangled Banner
20 Cents (5 Sgr.)

No. 2. American Banner.
25 Cents. (¼ Thlr.)

No. 3. Yankee doodle.
20 Cents. (5 Sgr.)

No. 4. Hail Columbia
20 Cents. (5 Sgr.)

/ Double Edition / to use / as a Piano (solo) piece as well as a piece for voice.

Separate title page. No date. Plate number 2664.

The title page has a large drawing of an eagle against a background of flags, branches, arrows, and stars, together with the words "E pluribus unum." Music, in B-flat major, and text fill pp. 2-3. Page 2 states: "Arranged by Bergman." Page 3 also has a Chorus for Soprano, Alto, Tenor, and Bass. Copy at James J. Fuld.

Julius Schuberth began his music publishing firm in 1826 in Hamburg and opened branches in Leipzig in 1832 and in New York in 1850. The plate number indicates a publication date of 1861-62. The prices on the title page of Silbergroschen (Sgr.) and Thaler (Thlr.) show that the edition was intended for sale in Germany as well as in the United States.

No. 66   [1861–1863]

National Songs. / A. FOR VOICE AND PIANO (The Piano Accpt. by Chs. Voss)....(ea) / B. FOR PIANO ALONE WITHOUT VARIATIONS BY CHs. VOSS. (ea) / C. do. WITH VARIATIONS do......(ea) / No. 1. Star spangd. Banner. No. 2. Hail Columbia. No. 3. Yankee Doodle. / OFFENBACH o/M, by JOHN ANDRÉ.

Separate title page. No date. No plate number.

The many-colored title page has a large drawing of an eagle against a background of the sun, together with the words "E PLURIBUS UNUM." Below is an American flag with 34 stars (1861–63). The verso of the title page is blank. Music, in B-flat major in 6/4, and text, engraved, fill pp. 3–4. Page 3 states "AMERICAN NATIONAL HYMN. / New and correct edition. arranget [sic] by Charles Voss." There is a Chorus for So-

prano, Alto, Tenor, and Basso on p. 5. There is no plate number, but at the foot of each music page appears "G. A. & Co." Copy at James J. Fuld.

Johann André began music publishing in Offenbach am Main in 1784.

A later variant, Muller No. 66A, is the same as the foregoing except that the music pages are not engraved and the verso of p. 5 advertises *Sonderkatalog No. 16*. Copy at James J. Fuld.

No. 67   **[1863]**

NOTED NOTES / *arranged for the* / Piano-Forte / *by* / NOTED AUTHORS
........25 cts

No. 1.–MARYLAND, MY MARYLAND ....25 cts.
No. 2.–NATIONAL MEDLEY   "
No. 3.–THY VOICE HATH A CHARM .... "
No. 4.–STAR-SPANGLED BANNER .... "
No. 5.–WE ARE COMING, FATHER ABRAHAM .... "
No. 6.–BANNER MARCH .. "
No. 7.–HER BRIGHT SMILE HAUNTS ME STILL .... "
No. 8.–FIRST LOVE REDOWA, ... "
No. 9.–HAUNTED STREAM   "
No. 10.–ROCHESTER SCHOTTISCHE .. "
No. 11.–VALLEY OF CHAMOUNI, ... "
No. 12.–MAIDEN'S PRAYER,   "
No. 13.–JUANITA, or, WANETA, ... "
No. 14.–CONGRESS GRAND MARCH, ... "
No. 15.–WHAT ARE THE WILD WAVES SAYING .. "
No. 16.–HURRAH STORM GALLOP, ... "

Copies of the above Pieces sent by mail, postage paid, upon receipt of the price as marked. / *Address the Publishers* / WINNER & CO., 933 SPRING GARDEN STREET, PHILADELPHIA

Collective title page. No date. No plate number.

Verso of title page blank.

Music and text fill pp. 3–5. The caption title on p. 3 reads: THE / STAR SPANGLED BANNER. Copy at Lester S. Levy.

The music is an arrangement for voice with piano accompaniment in 3/4 in C major.

Verso of p. 5 carries a comic musical engraving by Waitt, and lists thirty-two titles as: NEW MUSIC– – – –JUST PUBLISHED by WINNER & CO., / DEALERS IN / MUSIC

AND MUSICAL INSTRUMENTS / No. 933 Spring Garden Street, / PHILADELPHIA.

Septimus Winner was one of the most prolific song-writers of his period. He is best known for his *Listen to the Mocking Bird*, the words for which he wrote in 1855 under the pseudonym of Alice Hawthorne, his mother's maiden name. Winner commenced publishing music in 1850 at 257 and 267 Callowhill Street, Philadelphia, and remained in the music business at various Philadelphia addresses until his death in 1902.

No. 68   **[1864]**

THE STAR SPANGLED BANNER / THE AMERICAN NATIONAL LYRIC / SUNG BY / MRS. HOWARD PAUL

Separate title page. No date. No plate number.

Verso of title page is blank. The decorative title page is ornamented with a chromolithographed picture of Mrs. Paul, attired in symbolic costume and holding an American flag. On lower left margin of the picture appears the hand-lettered name "R. J. Hamerton," and below it "Stannard & Dixon." "R. J. Hamerton, lith." appears again in the lower right margin.

Music and text fill pp. 1–7.

The caption title on p. 1 reads: THE STAR-SPANGLED BANNER. / The Symphonies and Accompaniments by / FERDINAND WALLERSTEIN. Copy at Lester S. Levy.

The music is an arrangement for voice with piano accompaniment in 3/4 in C major.

Verso of p. 7 lists about eighty titles from: METZLER AND CO.'S / SELECT CATALOGUE / OF / NEW AND POPULAR SONGS. At bottom of verso appears: LONDON: METZLER & CO., 37, 38, 35 & 36, GREAT MARLBOROUGH STREET, W.

Another edition, Muller No. 68A, bears plate number 1547. Verso of p. 7 lists about one / NEW LIST OF SONGS. Copy at Lester S. Levy.

No. 69   1864-1865

CHOICE COLLECTION/OF/OLD AND NEW SONGS/BY VARIOUS AUTHORS

BOBBIN AROUND	Beckel 20	STAR SPANGLED BANNER	N. Song 30	
SHELLS OF OCEAN	Cherry 30	A DOLLAR OR TWO	Beckel 30	
JUANITA	Mrs. Norton 30	OFFICERS FUNERAL	Mrs. Norton 30	
EVER OF THEE	Foley Hall 30	HOME SWEET HOME	Bishop 30	
I CANNOT DANCE TO NIGHT	Mrs. Baily 30	MY HAPPY HOME	Hodson 30	
MOTHER IS THE BATTLE OVER	B. Roefs 30	WITHIN A MILE OF EDINBORO	Scotch Song 30	
HER BRIGHT SMILE	Wrighton 30	KATHLEEN MAVOURNEEN	Crouch 30	
ANNIE LAURIE	Scotch Song 30	THOU ART GONE FROM MY GAZE	Linley 30	
VALLEY OF CHAMOUNI	Glover 30	MARY OF ARGYLE	Nelson 30	
MY MOTHER DEAR	Lover 30			
IL BACIO	L. Arditi 50			
KATE DARLING	30			

SAINT LOUIS/Published by ENDRES & COMPTON 52 Fourth St.

Collective title page. No date. Plate number 152-3.

Verso of title page contains advertisement of POPULAR INSTRUMENTAL MUSIC /JUST PUBLISHED BY/ENDRES & COMPTON/52 FOURTH STREET, ST. LOUIS, DESCRIBING THIRTEEN PIECES AND LISTING SEVEN OTHERS.

Music and text fill pp. 3-5. The caption title on p. 3 reads STAR SPANGLED BANNER/AN AMERICAN NATIONAL HYMN/Duett song and Chorus/maestoso. Copy at The Free Library of Philadelphia.

The music with words of first two verses is an arrangement for two voices with piano accompaniment in 3/4 in C major. Last two lines of song, beginning "Oh! say does the Star Spangled" are repeated with accompaniment for four voices.

Words of third and fourth verses are at bottom of p. 5.

Verso of p. 5 contains list and description of 10 new songs published by Endres & Compton. Border, as well as border of verso of title page advertises COMPTON, ENDRES & CO.'S PIANO FORTES.